1000 Random Things You Always Believed That Are Not True

by
John Brown

Kindle Edition

* * * * *

Published by John Brown at Amazon
Kindle

MYTH 1. | *The Earth is orbiting around the Sun.* The Earth doesn't orbit around the Sun, it actually orbits around the Solar System's center of mass, known as the Barycenter. Although this point often falls within the mass of the Sun, it can also be shifted by the pull of other larger planets. Therefore, at least some of the time, everything in the solar system is orbiting around empty space.

MYTH 2. | *The tongue has different regions dedicated to different tastes.* The tongue doesn't have different regions dedicated to different tastes. Every single taste can be sensed on every part of your tongue.

MYTH 3. | *Returning baby birds to their nests causes their mothers to reject them.* Picking up baby birds and returning them to their nests will not cause their mothers to reject them.

MYTH 4. | *Sugar makes you hyper.* Sugar doesn't actually make you hyper, and the idea of a sugar rush is an urban myth. According to a recent study done by researchers at Yale University, the entire "rush" is a placebo effect that we get from believing that sugar will make us hyper.

MYTH 5. | *Chameleons change their colors to blend into their environment.* While chameleons often do change their color to match that of their environment, they do it in order to communicate.

MYTH 6. | *Napoleon was very short.* According to the average height of a French man, Napoleon was actually taller than the average.

MYTH 7. | *Vikings had horns on their helmets.* Vikings did not wear helmets with horns on them.

MYTH 8. | *Ingesting chewing gum will take 7 years to digest.* It doesn't take 7 years to digest chewing gum. In fact, it can't be digested at all and will simply pass right through you as is.

MYTH 9. | *People with red and blonde hair are going extinct.* Red heads and blondes aren't going extinct, they're just becoming more rare due to the world population increasing. In order for red heads or blondes to go extinct, every single person that carries that particular gene would have to die or not reproduce.

MYTH 10. | *Bats are blind. Bats aren't actually blind.* While some do use echolocation, they also have excellent night vision which allows them to see just as well as we see in the daylight.

MYTH 11. | *Life expectancy in the middle ages was low.* Life expectancy in the middle ages wasn't as low as many people think. The average age was brought down due to high infant mortality rates, however, most adults lived well into their late 60s.

MYTH 12. | *Fingers wrinkle because they absorb water.* Your fingers don't wrinkle because they absorbed water, they wrinkle because your brain sends them a message to. While many people aren't sure what the exact cause behind the wrinkling is, many researchers suspect it's to improve our grip on wet surfaces.

MYTH 13. | *The Coriolis effect changes the direction the toilet flushes.* The Coriolis effect doesn't change the direction the toilet flushes, it only affects very large bodies of water. If your toilet is flushing backwards, it's because the water enters the toilet backwards.

MYTH 14. | *The goldfish has a 3 second memory.* While the goldfish doesn't remember things like us, their memory is capable to absorb much more than 3 seconds of information.

MYTH 15. | *Sharks don't get cancer.* Just like any living thing, sharks do get cancer.

MYTH 16. | *Cracking your knuckles will lead to arthritis.* Cracking your knuckles won't lead to arthritis. In fact, a doctor did an experiment on himself by cracking his knuckles on one hand every day for sixty years to see if it would lead to arthritis.

In the end, it didn't and Donald Unger, the doctor, received the Medicine Prize from Ig Nobel Prizes.

MYTH 17. | *Dropping a penny from the top of the Empire State Building will kill someone.* Dropping a penny from the top of the Empire State Building will not kill anyone as the penny wouldn't be able to reach the necessary force to do any damage to a human being.

MYTH 18. | *Fingernails and hair continue to grow after death.* Fingernails and hair do not continue to grow after death, however the surrounding skin will start to recede which gives off the illusion that the nails are growing.

MYTH 19. | *Dogs sweat through their tongue.* Dogs don't sweat through their tongue since most of their sweat glands are located in their foot pads. While panting does help keep them cool, panting doesn't mean that they're sweating.

MYTH 20. | *You are born with all of the brain cells you will ever have.* You aren't born with all of the brain cells that you will ever have because your brain continues to grow and produce new cells in certain regions. This process is called neurogenesis.

MYTH 21. | *The color of the mucus in your nose indicates whether you have a bacterial or viral infection.* The color of the mucus in your nose doesn't have anything to do with indicating if you have a bacterial or viral infection as the color can vary due to a variety of different illnesses.

MYTH 22. | *Lightning doesn't strike the same spot twice.* Lightning can and does strike the same spot multiple times. In fact, the Empire State Building is struck up to 100 times a year.

MYTH 23. | *Lemmings follow each other and commit mass suicide.* Lemmings don't follow each other and commit mass suicide. This was wrongly created by a 1958 Disney documentary titled "White Wilderness," in which the filmmakers ran a pack of lemmings off a cliff in order to make an "entertaining" documentary.

MYTH 24. | *There are people who have a photographic memory.* There is no such thing as having a photographic memory. While there are people who have exceptional memories, they still can't recall events with as much detail as a photo taken with a camera.

MYTH 25. | *All people with Tourettes randomly yell out swear words.* Not all people with Tourettes randomly yell out swear words, only a very small percentage do. It's a lot more common for people with Tourettes to have involuntary movements and other sound tics than to just yell out profanity.

MYTH 26. | *Shaving your hair makes it thicker.* Shaving your hair doesn't make it thicker. While it might feel coarser, that's just because the ends are more blunt from being freshly shaved than from the hair being thicker.

MYTH 27. | *During the middle ages, many people thought the Earth was flat.* In fact, during the middle ages, most scholars knew that the Earth was round. The myth that people believed that the Earth was flat was started in the 1940s by the Members of the Historical Association.

MYTH 28. | *McDonald's burgers can't rot.* McDonald's burgers can and will rot under the right conditions in order for the processed foods to be broken down.

MYTH 29. | *Stress causes chronic high blood pressure.* While stress can temporarily increase blood pressure, the main causes of chronic high blood pressure are smoking, genetics and a bad diet.

MYTH 30. | *HIV transitioned from monkeys to humans through cross-species intercourse.* While the exact point of transfer of HIV from monkeys to humans is still unknown, it's a lot more likely that the virus jumped through hunting and ingesting monkeys than through cross-species intercourse.

MYTH 31. | *Ostriches stick their heads in the ground when they're scared.* Ostriches don't stick their heads in the ground when they're scared, they flop on the ground and play dead.

MYTH 32. | *The northern hemisphere of the Earth is closer to the Sun when it's summer.* The northern hemisphere of the Earth is not closer to the Sun when it's summer, it's just warmer in the summer because the northern hemisphere it tilted towards the Sun, which allows us to get hit with the Sun's rays directly.

MYTH 33. | *All diamonds are made from compressed coal.* Most diamonds aren't actually made from compressed coal, they're compressed and heated 90 miles below the surface of the Earth, while coal is found at about 2 miles below the Earth's surface.

MYTH 34. | *Dogs and cats see in grayscale.* Actually, dogs and cats don't see in grayscale, they see in different shades of blue and green.

MYTH 35. | *People use only 10% of their brain.* People use their entire brain, we just use different parts of the brain at different times.

MYTH 36. | *Frogs and toads give you warts.* Frogs and toads won't give you warts. Touching another person's warts will give you warts as the human papillomavirus is what causes most warts.

MYTH 37. | *Opossums hang by their tails.* A baby opossum can hang from its tail for a few seconds before it falls off, but an adult is too heavy.

MYTH 38. | *Searing meat seals in moisture.* Searing meat doesn't seal in moisture, it actually causes meat to lose its moisture. The actual value in searing your meat is that it creates a brown crust that is rich in flavor.

MYTH 39. | *Food that is cooked with wine or liquor is non-alcoholic.* A study found that when you cook your food with liquor, some of the alcohol still remains in the food. 25% of the liquor remains after one hour of baking or simmering, and 10% remains after two hours. However, eating a dish that's been prepared with alcohol will rarely contain sufficient amounts of alcohol to cause any level of intoxication.

MYTH 40. | *Sushi means raw fish.* Sushi doesn't mean raw fish and not all sushi includes raw fish in it. The name "sushi" simply refers to any dish that includes vinegared rice. In the traditional form of sushi in the Osaka region of Japan, all the ingredients are either cooked or cured and raw fish is never used.

MYTH 41. | *Microwave ovens cook food from the inside out.* Upon penetrating the outer layers of the food, microwave radiation mostly heats food at skin depth. For example, lean meat has a skin depth of about 1 centimeter and if you heat it in a microwave, only the first centimeter will really have any warmth in it.

MYTH 42. | *The Twinkie has an infinite shelf life.* In fact, the Twinkie has a shelf life of, approximately, 45 days. However, it generally remains on a store shelf for about 7 to 10 days.

MYTH 43. | *Fortune cookies came from China.* Despite being associated with Chinese cuisine in the United States, fortune cookies were brought in by the Japanese. The cookies are extremely rare in China, where they're actually seen as symbols of American cuisine.

MYTH 44. | *You must wait 24 hours before filing a missing person report.* It's extremely rare that you must wait 24 hours before filing a missing person report. In fact, if there is any evidence of violence or unusual absence, law enforcement agencies in the United States, stress the important of investigating as early as possible.

MYTH 45. | *The forbidden fruit in the Book of Genesis is an apple.* While the forbidden fruit that is mentioned in the Book of Genesis is widely assumed to be an apple, and is widely depicted as an apple in Western art, the Bible doesn't actually identify what type of fruit it is. The original Hebrew text mentions only the tree and fruit, while the early Latin translations use the word "mali", which translates into both "evil" and "apple". While all of Western art depicts the fruit as the apple, many Jewish scholars suggest that the fruit could just as easily have been a grape, a fig, wheat, an apricot or an etrog.

MYTH 46. | *The Buddha was obese.* The historical Buddha was not obese, and the "chubby Buddha" or the "laughing Buddha" is a 10th century Chinese folk hero called Budai. In Chinese Buddhist culture, Budai came to be revered as an incarnation of Maitreya, the Bodhisttva who will become a Buddha to restore Buddhism after the teachings of the historical Buddha, Siddhartha Guatama.

MYTH 47. | *Jesus was born on December 25th.* There is no evidence that Jesus was born on December 25th. The Bible never claims a date, but simply implies a date closer to September. The fixed date is attributed to Pope Julius the First because in the year 350 CE, he declared the twenty fifth of December the official date of celebration. The date might have been chosen to correspond with either the day exactly nine months after Christians believe Jesus to have been conceived.

MYTH 48. | *The black belt indicates mastery in martial arts.* The black belt doesn't necessarily indicate mastery in martial arts. The belt was first introduced for judo in the 1880s to indicate competency of all the basic techniques of the sport. Promotion beyond black belt varies among different martial arts. However, in judo, holders of higher ranks are awarded belts with alternating red and white panels, with the highest ranks having solid red belts.

MYTH 49. | *Swimming right after eating will give you a cramp.* Despite the common belief, there's no correlation between eating and cramping, and our bodies are well adapted to simultaneously swim and digest. You might get queasy if you exert yourself too quickly, but that has nothing to do with the water.

MYTH 50. | *In the United Kingdom, there's a rat within six feet of you wherever you go.* It's estimated that the United Kingdom has about 3.1 million rats in its urban areas. If the rats decided to spread out as widely as possible, there would be one rat every 5,000 square meters in London. Therefore, you would actually be 164 feet from one, wherever you went.

MYTH 51. | *You can see the Great Wall of China from space.* Even from a very low orbit of the International Space Station, the Great Wall is impossible to make out. While this myth is still found in old school textbooks, it was actually disproven by one of China's own astronauts, Yang Liwei.

MYTH 52. | *Van Gogh cut his own ear off.* Many historians actually believe that the ear injury was inflicted by Van Gogh's friend and fellow artist, Paul Gaugin.

MYTH 53. | *Poinsettias are lethal.* The myth was started sometime in the 20the century, right after they were brought to the United States from Mexico. Allegedly, the child of a military officer died when he consumed a poinsettia leaf. As a result, the rumor that the flower is toxic spread. However, the most that will happen to you if you ingest poinsettia leaves is an upset stomach.

MYTH 54. | *Humans have 5 senses.* This is widely critiqued by scholars, especially by Harvard Medical School researchers. Many of them believe that humans have much more than 5 senses, some of which include: equilibrioception, nociception, proprioception, thermoception, intercoception, etc.

MYTH 55. | *Hydrogen Peroxide helps wounds heal.* Hydrogen Peroxide doesn't help your wounds heal. The bubbling that you see when you apply it to a wound is the solution attacking you. It causes cellular damage and makes it even harder for the wound to heal properly.

MYTH 56. | *If you cut an earthworm in half, it will regenerate into two earthworms.* While earthworms do regenerate, they won't divide into two entirely new earthworms. What happens is that the front of the worm lives and the back dies. The regeneration happens when the front of the worm replaces the lost back end of its body.

MYTH 57. | *You should drink 8 glasses of water every day.* The amount of water a person should drink varies wildly from each individual. For example, if you do plenty of physical labor then you should be drinking much more than 8 glasses of water.

MYTH 58. | *Columbus discovered the Earth was round.* Actually that fact was common knowledge in Columbus' day and it's what prompted him to attempt to sail around the world to reach the Orient in the first place.

MYTH 59. | *The theory of evolution proposes that humans evolved from apes.* This is actually a very common misconception. The theory actually proposes that humans and apes shared a common, now extinct ancestor, not that one evolved from the other.

MYTH 60. | *An apple falling on his head is what gave Isaac Newton the key to identifying gravity.* Though Newtown was partially responsible for the creation of this myth, he never really claimed that the apple fell on his head nor did he make any discoveries that would lead him to develop the theory of universal gravitation until nearly 20 years later.

MYTH 61. | *Caffeinated drinks dehydrate you.* If you were only consuming caffeine, it might dehydrate you to some degree but the water that is contained in most caffeinated drinks offsets that effect.

MYTH 62. | *Bulls hate the color red.* Bulls are actually color blind and generally react to the bull fighter's waving of the cloth rather than the actual color of the cloth.

MYTH 63. | *You should never wake a sleepwalker.* All that will happen if you wake up a sleepwalker is that they'll experience confusion for a couple of seconds until they come to. However, it's a lot safer to wake them than to let them wander around unconscious.

MYTH 64. | *Camels store water in their humps.* Camel humps are actually large mounds of fat, not water containers, which allow them to survive in extreme temperatures for long periods of time.

MYTH 65. | *Koalas are bears.* Koalas are sometimes referred to as "koala bear", but this is a false nickname. They're actually marsupials and have no relation to bears.

MYTH 66. | *Cows lie down when it's about to rain.* Cows can't predict weather conditions and the reason they lie down is often to chew their cud or just relax.

MYTH 67. | *Porcupines shoot their quills at an enemy.* Porcupines can't propel their quills from their bodies, much like we can't shoot our fingernails at people.

MYTH 68. | *Cats have nine lives.* This myth probably originated from the Egyptian Gods and religions, where the Sun God Atum-Ra, one of the Ennead, or the Nine, would assume the form of a cat when visiting the underworld. Throughout history, cats were seen as magical and otherworldly creatures, and their resilience in surviving high falls and long confinements without sustenance is what perpetrated the myth of a cat having nine lives.

MYTH 69. | *Cats purr only when they're happy.*
Purring is one of the first sounds a kitten can make.
Kittens can purr by the time they're 48 hours old and,
while nursing, both mother cat and the kittens can be
heard to be purring. However, while purring is often
heard at time of contentment, cats are also known to
purr when they're in pain or when they're about to die.

MYTH 70. | *Sloths are lazy.* Researchers have found
that wild sloths sleep for only 10 hours a day.
However, the sloths are held captive in zoos sleep up
to 16 hours a day, sometimes even more, because
they don't need to stay awake to find food.

MYTH 71. | *Rattlesnakes rattle their tail before they
attack their pray.* Rattlesnakes only rattle their tail
when they're frightened. Doing so, alerts predators
around them to their presence so they are very careful
where they step. However, they definitely don't want
to warn their prey before striking it.

MYTH 72. | *The chance of a coin landing on heads
rather than tails is fifty-fifty.* The chance of a coin
landing on heads isn't fifty-fifty. It all depends on if
the coins is faced heads up to begin with, as it's more
likely to land on heads. Students at Stanford
University recorded thousands of coin tosses with
high-speed cameras and discovered that the chances
are approximately fifty-one to forty-nine.

MYTH 73. | *Gladiators fought to the death.*
Gladiators didn't kill each other as often as everyone

thinks. The most prized gladiators were worth a lot of money and they were trained as entertainers, with many living very long lives. A grave found at Ephesus in modern day Turkey in 2007, found the remains of 67 men aged 20 - 30, many sustaining serious wounds but they all healed over time, suggesting that each one of those men was a prized fighter with access to top of the line medical care at the time.

MYTH 74. | *King Arthur was a real person.* While there are mentions in history of a person named Arthur living in England around the late 5th and early 6th century, there's never any mention of him being a king. He's mentioned in the 9th century Historia Brittonum as having taken part in a bloody battle at Mount Badon, and in the Annalaes Cambriae, but the 6th century writer, Gildas, who wrote about the battle, doesn't mention Arthur at all. He's also completely absent from the Anglo-Saxon Chronicle, which is the best guide we have on the happenings of that time.

MYTH 75. | *Witches were burned at Salem Witch Trials.* The Salem trials in 1692 and 1693 were a terrifying affair, but despite the images of witches being burned, this didn't happen. What did happen is that, most of the 20 people who were convicted, were hanged. Many of those who survived were imprisoned. By that point in time, burning people alive was illegal in England and was also banned in the new American colonies.

MYTH 76. | *Edison invented the light bulb.* Thomas Edison invented many other things, but the first electric light bulb wasn't it. Several people had invented light bulbs before him, but Edison was the first one who brought out the longer lasting incandescent versions that become commercially available.

MYTH 77. | *Einstein was bad at math.* Einstein was actually brilliant from an early age. What did happen is that he failed his entrance exam to the Swiss Polytechnic in Zurich, despite excelling in the math and physics sections, because he was 16 years old, two years younger than most people who applied for university.

MYTH 78. | *Humans have stopped evolving.* Humans are actually evolving biologically every single day. For example, 2,000 years ago, most humans couldn't consume milk past the age of five. Then, around 10,000 B.C. near modern day Turkey, a genetic mutation in one human changed the entire lactose production. The gene passed over to other people and, over the next few thousand years, it continued to spread, allowing the majority of people in the Eurasia region to drink milk their entire lives.

MYTH 79. | *You lose most of your body heat through your head.* Actually, if you were completely naked, you would lose the same amount of body heat everywhere equally. The fact that this myth managed to last so long is because your head is less likely to be covered than other parts of your body.

MYTH 80. | *One human year is equivalent to seven dog years.* Actually, the amount of dog years that one human year is equal to varies widely between the size and the breed of the dog.

MYTH 81. | *Vitamin C is good for treating a cold.* Most researchers and experts say that there is little to no actual evidence that supports this.

MYTH 82. | *Penguins mate for life.* While penguins are mostly monogamous, there are some species, such as the Emperor Penguin, which is only monogamous for the season.

MYTH 83. | *There is a dark side of the Moon.* There isn't any one place on the Moon that's always in the dark. The moon constantly rotates on its own axis, which means that every area on the moon is dark at some point in time.

MYTH 84. | *Sunflowers track the Sun across the sky.* Actually, the uniform alignment of the flowers results from what's called "heliotropism" at the bud stage, which is before the appearance of flower heads.

MYTH 85. | *Frankenstein was the name of the monster in Mary Shelley's famous book.* Frankenstein was actually the name of the monster's creator, Dr. Frankenstein, and the monster didn't actually have a name.

MYTH 86. | *Microwave radiation causes cancer.*
Most experts say that microwave ovens don't give off
enough energy to damage DNA in cells so they can't
cause cancer.

MYTH 87. | *Houseflies live for only 24 hours.* Adult
houseflies can live up to one month in the wild, with
some living for up to two months.

MYTH 88. | *Eating cheese before bed will give you
nightmares.* Cheese is widely believed to give you
more emotionally charged dreams but that doesn't
necessarily mean that you'll have nightmares.

MYTH 89. | *The capital of Australia is Sydney.* The
capital of Australia is actually Canberra and not
Sydney.

MYTH 90. | *Going out in the cold with wet hair will
make you sick.* While you might feel cold, there's no
evidence that supports the myth that you will get sick.

MYTH 91. | *Alcohol keeps you warm.* A drink or
two will cause your blood vessels to dilate, moving
warm blood closer to the surface of your skin, which
makes you feel warmer temporarily. However, you
will lose core body heat at the same time.

MYTH 92. | *Electrons revolve around the nucleus of
an atom.* Electrons don't orbit the nucleus in neat little
elliptical paths, instead, they undulate around the
nucleus in a complex series of ripples.

MYTH 93. | *Raindrops have a teardrop shape.* Raindrops are actually shaped more like kidney beans or very small hamburger buns.

MYTH 94. | *There is no gravity in space.* Gravity can be found everywhere in the solar system. On Earth, we feel gravity because it's pulling us towards the core. In space, shuttles are in a constant state of free-fall towards the Earth, so astronauts appear weightless because they are falling at the same speed that the shuttle is falling.

MYTH 95. | *Many people beat murder convictions by pleading insanity.* This defense is very rarely used and even when it is used, it usually fails. If it succeeds, the defendant is almost always previously diagnosed as mentally ill and is already on strong medication.

MYTH 96. | *A defibrillator is used to restart the heart.* The defibrillator is actually used to stop the heart that is beating incorrectly, in the hope of restarting it to beat properly.

MYTH 97. | *CPR is used to restart the heart.* CPR isn't used to restart the heart, it's used to keep circulation of blood going until medical professionals get to the scene.

MYTH 98. | *You swallow eight spiders a year in your sleep.* This myth was faked as part of an article about how easy it is for a convincing sounding "fact" to be accepted as true.

MYTH 99. | *There is no Nobel Prize for mathematics because a mathematician was having an affair with Alfred Nobel's wife.* Firstly, Nobel was never married. Secondly, Nobel established prizes for fields that interested him, and mathematics simply wasn't among them.

MYTH 100. | *A special compound can be added to the water in swimming pools to reveal the presence of urine.* Experts on chemicals used in public swimming pools say that although a reliable urine detecting dye can be produced, getting it to react only to urine and no trigger in the presence of similar organic compounds would make the mixture very difficult to produce and thus, very expensive to sell. Currently, there isn't any company that is working on creating the compound, nor is there any company that plans to create the compound.

MYTH 101. | *Milk is essential to your overall health.* Milk is just one of many different sources for calcium and Vitamin D.

MYTH 102. | *Tar and nicotine in cigarettes cause cancer.* Excessive smoke in your lungs is what causes cancer. The Radon and Polonium in the smoke is enough to account for almost all cases of cigarette related lung cancer.

MYTH 103. | *Being overworked can cause a nervous breakdown.* Nervous breakdowns don't even appear as an official mental health disorder in the DSM-IV.

MYTH 104. | *Male masturbation is unhealthy.* Research has shown that masturbating early and often may reduce the chance of prostate cancer later in life.

MYTH 105. | *Females are biologically inferior in math and spatial skills.* Statistically, males and females have very similar grade averages in math courses from grade school through doctorate level classes. However, male enrollment in math specific programs is drastically higher than female enrollment.

MYTH 106. | *Based on global warming, Earth will be hotter in 2,000 years.* Nothing is for certain, but researchers believe that in this kind of complex nonlinear system, the chance of us having another ice age is just as likely as the Earth being much hotter in the coming 2,000 years.

MYTH 107. | *Biodiesel is better than gasoline.* Biodiesel is more expensive, increases the overall cost of food and still pollutes the environment in much the same way as gasoline.

MYTH 108. | *Herbal medicine is healthier than modern medicine.* In many studies, herbal medicine has been shown to have either no effect on an illness or an undesirable side effect.

MYTH 109. | *Highly social people are psychologically healthier.* Highly social people are not in any way healthier than non social people; however, they are usually happier.

MYTH 110. | *Nutritional supplements make you live longer.* While nutritional supplements are great for supplementing a healthy diet, they will not make you live longer. In fact, due to many people misusing supplements, they end up doing more harm than good.

MYTH 111. | *The Big Bang was an explosion.* The Big Bang was actually an expansion of space, not an explosion.

MYTH 112. | *Weight belts prevent injuries.* If used properly when lifting large amounts of weight, they do help stabilize your body and prevent injury. The real problem is that most beginner weight lifters swing their bodies and hyper-extend their backs while lifting with their upper body. When they wear a weight belt for upper body exercises, they still swing their bodies, only this time, they use more weight because they feel that they can lift more with the belt and injuries become much more severe.

MYTH 113. | *Soap kills germs.* Plain hand soap doesn't kill germs. What it does do is it lifts the germs off the surface of your skin, forcing them to be washed down the drain.

MYTH 114. | *Alcohol is a great antiseptic for open wounds.* Alcohol is a great disinfectant for intact skin and inanimate objects; however, alcohol is not effective when applied to open wounds. When it's used on open and exposed tissue, alcohol actually kills some of the human tissue along with the germs. This can delay the healing process of larger wounds.

MYTH 115. | *Fructose is healthier than sucrose.* Sucrose, or table sugar, is made from sugarcane. Fructose is usually made from corn or fruits and is a cheaper alternative to sucrose. At one point, it was thought that fructose was healthier, but researchers have recently discovered that it comes with many negatives. Some of these negatives include cholesterol increases and digestion difficulty, in addition to it converting to fat far more easily than any other type of sugar.

MYTH 116. | *You can't fold a piece of paper more than seven times.* You can actually fold a piece of paper up to 12 times.

MYTH 117. | *George Washington had wooden teeth.* George Washington lost his teeth in his 20s; however, his dentures weren't made out of wood. He had four sets of dentures that were made from gold, hippopotamus ivory, lead and a mixture of human and animal teeth.

MYTH 118. | *Eggs are bad for your heart.* While eggs do contain a large amount of cholesterol in their yolks, and cholesterol does clog our arteries, labeling eggs as bad for your heart is simply wrong. Professor of nutrition at Penn State University, Penny Kris-Etherton, even noted that, "Epidemiologic studies show that most healthy people can eat an egg a day without problems."

MYTH 119. | *Wild dolphins are friendly and will save humans in trouble.* Dolphins don't actually care about humans. The myth that wild dolphins are friendly and will come to your assistance when you're in trouble is absolutely false. In fact, many people have been bitten or injured while attempting to swim with wild dolphins.

MYTH 120. | *Owls are the wisest birds.* The earliest known link between owls and wisdom comes from their association with Athena, the Greek goddess of wisdom. However, owls are actually placed on the lower end of intelligent birds, with the common crow being considered the wisest among birds.

MYTH 121. | *If you keep a goldfish in a dark room, it will eventually turn white.* The goldfish will actually get paler, but it won't turn completely white. Fish produce pigment in response to light, much like we do, but they also get some pigment from the food that they eat. Therefore, even if they're left in the dark forever, they wouldn't go completely white.

MYTH 122. | *1 out of every 20 people have an extra rib.* The actual figure seems to be around 1 in every 200 people.

MYTH 123. | *There is enough gold on Earth for every person in the world to own about 5 golden rings.* Estimates of the amount of gold in the world range from 155,244 to 2.5 million tonnes. A single ring uses about 5.5g of gold and there are about 7 billion people in the world. Roughly, that would give you between 4 and 64 gold rings per person.

MYTH 124. | *Scientists estimate that 86% of all land creatures and 91% of sea creatures remain undiscovered.* This myth was actually misinterpreted from a PLOS Biology paper in which the authors say: "Our results suggest that some 86% of the species on Earth, and 91% in the ocean, still await description." This is completely different than saying that they remain undiscovered.

MYTH 125. | *Eating a lot of fruit is healthy.* Actually, fruit has a lot of fructose, a type of sugar, which is not good in large quantities. Excessive sugar, no matter where it comes from, is still bad for your body. However, if you have a choice between a chocolate bar or a fruit, the fruit is still better due to the nutrients that it has alongside the sugar.

MYTH 126. | *The legal drinking age in the United Kingdom is 18.* The legal drinking age, for drinking at a pub, in the United Kingdom is 18; however, if you can get someone else to purchase the alcohol for you, you can drink it at home at the age of 5 or older.

MYTH 127. | *Rats caused the Black Death.*
Actually, it was squirrels. Marmot squirrels from Mongolia spread the plague, as they were prone to the disease. Once the rats became infected as well, the disease became harder to eradicate due to such a large population of rats living in urban European cities.

MYTH 128. | *Slavery has been illegal in the United Kingdom for decades.* Slavery became illegal in the United Kingdom on April 6th, 2010. However, the status of slavery had never even existed under common law in England.

MYTH 129. | *The map of the world is perfectly accurate.* It's almost impossible to convey a 3D object on a 2D scale. The Mercator Map that we are used to seeing isn't the most accurate map but it is the easiest one for us to process, which is why it's the most common one to see.

MYTH 130. | *One day lasts exactly 24 hours.* Each day varies in length. For example, some days can last 50 seconds longer while others will be 50 seconds shorter. Time can never be exact because it all varies on the Earth's rotation, the tides, the weather, and geological events that take place around the planet.

MYTH 131. | *The Earth is a sphere.* While we see the Earth represented as a sphere, it's actually more of

an oval shape. It has bulges at the equator and the North and South pole are almost perfectly flat.

MYTH 132. | *If the planet's magnetic poles reversed, all life on Earth would perish.* Actually, the magnetic poles reverse themselves every few thousand years. The shifting of the poles does have an effect on the sea and the weather but nothing close to a cataclysmic event occurred.

MYTH 133. | *All of the continents used to be merged together to form Pangaea, a supercontinent.* While this is true, there have been seven other supercontinents in the Earth's existence. They are: Vaalbra, Ur, Kenorland, Columbia, Rodinia, Pannotia, and the earliest one we know, Pangaea. Scientists believe that another supercontinent will form in 100 million years and it'll be called Ultima.

MYTH 134. | *If you shoot the tank of a car, it'll explode.* This myth became famous with the help of Hollywood movies. In fact, for the car to explode by shooting the tank, the tank must be filled with more gas than gasoline because the gas will ignite from a hot bullet while the gasoline might not.

MYTH 135. | *The 100 Years War lasted for 100 years.* The 100 Years War actually lasted for 116 years and not 100 years.

MYTH 136. | *Winston Churchill became a revered war hero after World War II.* While Churchill's approval rating was high during the war, when he insisted that Britain needed to invade Russia now that they were recovering from the war, his approval rating plummeted. England was still trying to recover from the war and the last thing the people wanted was to start another one. Churchill was forced to retire immediately after World War II.

MYTH 137. | *Concentration camps were a creation of the Nazis.* Actually, the Spanish came up with the idea in 1895 to control their civilian population. The conditions weren't as brutal as Auschwitz but the civilians were still held there against their will.

MYTH 138. | *Hitler killed more people than anyone else in history.* In total, Hitler was responsible for up to 17 million deaths. Joseph Stalin was responsible for killing 23 million people, many of which were his own people. Mao Zedong of China killed as many as 78 million during his reign, many of which were also his own people.

MYTH 139. | *Hitler was a vegetarian.* Hitler ate more vegetables than meat due to his terrible digestive system, however, he still ate meat from time to time.

MYTH 140. | *The Ancient Mayans disappeared almost instantly.* Actually, their number dwindled over hundreds of years. They've taken hits from civil wars, droughts, disease, and deforestation.

MYTH 141. | *Amelia Earhart mysteriously vanished.* The mystery behind her sudden disappearance was solved just four years after she went missing. Her plane was found to be crashed near an island in Kiribati and her skeletal remains were found close by as well. The skeleton matched her measurements. They also found her equipment near the wreckage.

MYTH 142. | *No one knows who built the Easter Island Heads.* Actually, Easter Island was inhabited by a primitive tribe called the Rapa Nui. The tribe constructed the massive statues 400 years ago by cutting down their trees and rolling the boulders down to a location where they wanted to build the statues. Eventually, they destroyed their entire forest and stripped the soil of its nutrients. With no source of food left, they resorted to cannibalism.

MYTH 143. | *A plane's black box is black.* Originally, it was black but they changed it to orange in 1965 so it was easier to find after a plane crash.

MYTH 144. | *An EMP can shut down all electronics.* If an EMP came from a manmade bomb or from a solar flare, electronics such as computer and televisions would stop working for a brief moment but then they would be back to normal. The worst that could happen is that a power grid would go out and would have to be replaced. However, there is no single incident that could disable all technology in a massive area such as a large city and definitely not a large country.

MYTH 145. | *A DNA analysis that police forensics use can be done in a couple of minutes.* Due to the complexity of DNA, the most advanced Genetic Analyzer in the world would take well over 12 hours, and sometimes even 24 hours, to analyze a single strand of DNA.

MYTH 146. | *The Amish don't use electricity.* The Amish actually use solar power, artificial light, and batteries for their various household and business appliances.

MYTH 147. | *You can hack a computer in seconds.* This myth has been popularized by various Hollywood movies, however, the truth is much less appealing. Hacking a single computer can sometimes take hours to days of trial and error.

MYTH 148. | *Turning off the sound on your iPhone will help extend the battery life.* An iPhone actually uses more energy when the sound is turned off. When you get a text or a call, if your phone vibrates instead of making a sound, the amount of kinetic energy needed to make your phone move requires far more energy than emitting a sound.

MYTH 149. | *The police need to keep a criminal on the phone for as long as possible in order to trace the call.* Actually, it takes a few seconds for emergency response units to trade a call back to where it originated from.

MYTH 150. | *Online dating sites are full of perverts.* Recent research into online dating profiles has found that the most common job that a person with an online dating profile has is a teacher. Also, the researchers have found that more and more people are using online platforms to find relationships.

MYTH 151. | *Apple's iMac desktops and laptops can't get viruses.* While viruses and malware on iMacs are rare, they still exist and can be just as damaging as the ones found on the PC.

MYTH 152. | *The Vikings were a nation.* The Vikings were never one nation, but a collection of different tribes of warriors, explorers and merchants. During the era of Vikings, Scandinavia was separated into small areas where a chieftain ruled over his tribe.

MYTH 153. | *Vapes and e-cigarettes are a good substitute for cigarettes.* The entire logic behind e-cigarettes is that you can get your nicotine fix without the lung damaging tar found in cigarettes. However, e-cigarettes and vapes contain formaldehyde and acetone, which can cause eye disorders, respiratory problems, and cancer. The side effects from e-cigarettes are also more common than those of real cigarettes. For example, over 200 reports occur every month in the United States that involve children feeling sick after inhaling the vapor from e-cigarettes.

MYTH 154. | *A door bursting open on a plane would cause the entire aircraft to be torn apart.* If a window or door were to burst open on a plane, it would cause suction until the pressure stabilized in the cabin after a few seconds. The people that were next to the door or window would get sucked out, but the plane wouldn't rip apart.

MYTH 155. | *If a plane crashed, the survival rate would be extremely low.* Actually, from 1983 to 2000, there have been 53,487 people in plane crashes in the United States. Out of those 53,487 people, only 2,280 died; that's less than 4%.

MYTH 156. | *Floating in space without a spacesuit and oxygen mask would make you explode.* Space doesn't make your head explode, nor does it make your eyes swell up and burst. If you were floating in space without a suit, you would first experience yourself begin to freeze, followed by suffocation. It's very likely that you would first suffocate then freeze completely.

MYTH 157. | *Saturn and Uranus are the only planets that have rings.* Jupiter and Neptune also have rings but they are too faint to see.

MYTH 158. | *When a star dies, it turns into a black hole.* Only very large stars that die turn into black holes. For example, when our Sun dies in a few billion years, it will collapse into itself and turn into a white dwarf.

MYTH 159. | *The first animal in space was a dog.* The first animal in space was a fruit fly. Fruit flies were originally sent into space in 1946 to test radioactive exposure. This was done to gauge if humans could survive space. Eleven years after that, Laika the dog was sent into space.

MYTH 160. | *Coins have a metallic smell to them.* The smell isn't actually the coins, it's you. Human perspiration mixes with the iron of a coin and creates the distinct smell that people say smells like "metal". People also get a similar smell when blood comes into contact with skin because blood contains iron.

MYTH 161. | *Copper is the best conductor.* Silver is the best conductor but, due to its cost, many resort to using copper, which is much cheaper and still conducts electricity very well.

MYTH 162. | *Atoms are the smallest things in the universe.* Protons and neutrons that make up the nucleus of the atom are smaller than the atom. However, the edges of the atom are covered with an even smaller particle called electron. Smaller still, we have neutrinos, which are subatomic particles with no electrical mass. To put things into scale, a neutrino is so small that if an atom was the size of the Solar System, a neutrino would be the size of a golf ball.

MYTH 163. | *Air is mostly made up of oxygen.* 78% of the air that we breathe is actually nitrogen, and only 21% of is oxygen.

MYTH 164. | *All metals are magnetic.* Only four metals are magnetic and they are: nickel, iron, gadolinium and cobalt.

MYTH 165. | *Meth can be blue just like in the popular television show, Breaking Bad.* It's impossible for meth to be blue, unless you added a coloring agent to it. The chemical disposition of meth limits its color choices. Changing the chemical disposition would have a adverse effect on its potency.

MYTH 166. | *Clones look identical.* If you cloned an animal five times, there's a good chance that you will have five different looking animals. In an experiment done on a cat called Rainbow, her DNA was taken and a clone was created, called Copycat. Surprisingly, Copycat looked nothing alike in color or pattern to the original cat.

MYTH 167. | *Buddhism is common in India.* Less than 1% of Indians are Buddhists. There are a lot more Christians and Hindus in India, than Buddhists.

MYTH 168. | *The Star of David is a Jewish symbol.* The Star of David was a symbol in Buddhism, Hinduism, and Jainism before the Jewish religion popularized it amongst its followers.

MYTH 169. | *Hades, the Greek God of the Underworld, was evil.* Hades acted more like a judge in the underworld than an evil being who presided over it. In fact, he was far more reasonable in Greek mythology than his two brothers, Poseidon and Zeus, who killed far more people. Hades was given the rule of the Underworld and he governed and judged all souls, not just the evil ones. In Greek mythology, he was said to be passive and stern rather than pure evil, like Satan.

MYTH 170. | *Muslims don't believe in Jesus Christ.* Jesus Christ is mentioned several times in the Qur'an, as well as other Biblical characters such as Noah, Abraham, Adam and Even Mary.

MYTH 171. | *All Muslim women wear hijabs or burkhas.* Only some Muslim women choose to wear them, but there are many who remain with their Muslim faith but who choose not to wear either.

MYTH 172. | *The disciples of Jesus Christ wrote the Bible.* Actually, the Council of Nicea wrote the Bible.

MYTH 173. | *The Bible was written shortly after the death of Jesus Christ.* The Bible was written in 325 AD, which is three centuries after Christ's death.

MYTH 174. | *Thomas Jefferson freed all of his slaves while on his deathbed.* Thomas Jefferson could have freed as many as 800 slaves but he only freed 5 before he died.

MYTH 175. | *George Washington was the first president of America.* Peyton Randolph was the first American President but he was forgotten due to a technicality. When he was President, the United States was called The United Colonies of America.

MYTH 176. | *Trees create most of the oxygen on Earth.* While this is a common myth, it's actually algae that provides 90% of all the oxygen on the planet.

MYTH 177. | *Mushrooms are plants.* Mushrooms are fungi. Mushrooms have a DNA that's closer to an animal than a plant. Strangely enough, mushrooms have more genetic similarities to human beings than to any tree or flower.

MYTH 178. | *The largest living thing is the Sequoia tree.* There is a mushroom in Oregon that is largely underground, but spans 2,200 acres or 3.5 square miles.

MYTH 179. | *You can tell how old a tree is by cutting it and seeing how many rings it has on the inside.* This only applies to non-tropical trees. Many tropical trees don't have any rings on the inside. The only way to gauge how old those trees are is with radiocarbon dating.

MYTH 180. | *The capital of Brazil is Rio de Janeiro.* The capital of Brazil is actually Brasilia.

MYTH 181. | *The Pyramids of Giza are hundreds of miles away from civilization.* The busy city of Giza is only a few miles away from the pyramids. There are pizza franchises located on the strip across the pyramids where you can see them while you're ordering your food.

MYTH 182. | *The tallest mountain in Europe is Mont Blanc.* Until recently, Mount Elbrus was thought to be in Asia but it is actually in Europe, and at the very edge of Asia. Since Mount Elbrus is 5,632m high, it makes it the tallest mountain in Europe.

MYTH 183. | *England has the world's oldest parliament.* Iceland has the oldest parliament, dating back to 930 AD.

MYTH 184. | *Christmas trees originate from the United States.* Actually, Christmas trees originate from Germany in the 16th century.

MYTH 185. | *The longest waterfall in the world is Niagara Falls.* Angel Falls in Venezuela is the longest waterfall in the world. It's 17 times longer than Niagara Falls.

MYTH 186. | *The most common language in the world is English.* While 500 million people speak

English worldwide, nearly 2 billion people speak Mandarin in Asia.

MYTH 187. | *People from the United Kingdom have bad teeth.* There was a study done in 2006 that measured the amount of decayed, missing or filled teeth in the average 12 year old in Europe. The study found that Poland was the country with the worst dental care and the United Kingdom was considered to have the best teeth in Europe.

MYTH 188. | *South Africa has the highest production of diamonds.* Russia has the highest worldwide production of diamonds at 22.4% while South Africa is fifth with 9%.

MYTH 189. | *Japan exports more soy sauce than any other country.* The Netherlands export more soy sauce than Japan.

MYTH 190. | *Cocaine and heroin are the most common drugs Americans overdose on.* More Americans overdose on prescription painkillers like oxycontin than heroin and cocaine combined.

MYTH 191. | *Egypt has more pyramids than any other country in the world.* Actually, Sudan has the most pyramids than any other country in the world with at least 35 pyramids.

MYTH 192. | *Crucifixion hasn't been a means of torture for centuries.* Crucifixion is still carried out in Sudan.

MYTH 193. | *Japan has the highest life expectancy.* The average life expectancy in Japan is 83 years old. The country with the highest life expectancy is actually Monaco, with 90 years old.

MYTH 194. | *The United States is the most dangerous country in the world.* The United States is the eight most dangerous country with 15,000 murders per year. On the other hand, India is rated the most dangerous country in the world with over 43,000 murders per year.

MYTH 195. | *Walt Disney's first animated character was Mickey Mouse.* Walt Disney first created Oswald the Lucky Rabbit. While it was successful at first, he lost the rights to the character to Universal Studios. Then he came up with a cartoon mouse called Mortimer. Realizing that the name wouldn't resonate with his audience, he changed the name to Mickey.

MYTH 196. | *Gandhi was a pacifist.* While Gandhi didn't like violence, he said that it should be used when it was absolutely necessary. He even volunteered to fight in the Zulu War and World War I.

MYTH 197. | *Gypsies originated from Romania.*
Although the 10 million gypsies that currently reside
in Europe are from Romania, they didn't originate
there. Gypsies originated from India more than a
thousand years ago, then they spread through the
Middle-East through Iran and moved towards Europe
through Turkey. Eventually, they settled in Romania.

MYTH 198. | *Eskimos kiss by rubbing their noses
together.* Eskimos don't rub their noses together, but
they do get as close to the person as possible, to be
able to smell them. When there's a powerful blizzard
outside, Eskimos can't recognize each other's faces,
but they can recognize another person scent.

MYTH 199. | *Captain Cook discovered Australia.*
An English pirate called William Dampier and two
Dutchmen called Abel Tasman and Dirk Hartog
found Australia before Cook.

MYTH 200. | *The Mayan Civilization is extinct.*
There are 7 million Mayans still living in Mexico and
Guatemala. While some of them live on the outskirts
of society, a large percentage of them are completely
assimilated into modern life.

MYTH 201. | *Elvis Presley had black hair.* Elvis
used to dye his hair black for most of his career. His
real hair color was blonde.

MYTH 202. | *St. Patrick was Irish.* St. Patrick was
either Welsh or Scottish. He was kidnapped and

shipped to Ireland at 16 as a slave. His real name was
Maewyn Succat but, when he became a priest years
later, he took the name Patrick to honor Saint
Patricius.

MYTH 203. | *Gandhi's first name was Mahatma.*
His first name was actually Mohandas. Mahatma was
his title and it meant the "great soul".

MYTH 204. | *Rosa Parks was the first black woman
to refuse to sit at the back of the bus.* Actually,
Claudette Colvin was the first black woman to refuse
to give up her seat but, black activists refused to use
her as an example of equality because she was a
pregnant and unmarried teenager. Rosa Parks, on the
other hand, was a simple woman with no sort of
background; therefore, she was a perfect example for
their cause.

MYTH 205. | *Mozart's middle name was Amadeus.*
Mozart did have a nickname of Amade, but he was
never called Amadeus.

MYTH 205. | *Michael Jackson had long hair.*
During a Pepsi commercial, a pyrotechnic
malfunction burned Jackson's hair off entirely. He
had to wear a wig until the day he died.

MYTH 207. | *Michael Jackson had surgery to make
him white.* Michael Jackson had a pigmentation
disorder called vitiligo. Due to the disorder, his skin
color became patchy and he had his skin bleached in

order to even it out. An autopsy done at Jackson's death even confirmed that he had vitiligo.

MYTH 208. | *Michael Jackson invented the moonwalk.* Bill Bailey, a musician in 1955, invented the dance move.

MYTH 209. | *The popular movie "The Texas Chainsaw Massacre" is based on a true story.* The movie's main villain, "Leatherface" was inspired by a real life serial killer called Ed Gein. However, the events that took place in the movie never actually took place in the real life.

MYTH 210. | *Hollywood is the world's biggest distributor of movies.* India's Bollywood is a far larger movie distributor, followed by Nigeria. Hollywood is in third place.

MYTH 211. | *Mental institutions use straitjackets.* By law, mental institutions have to use the least restrictive method of restraint possible. This means that when patients lash out against the staff, they will often be sedated with medication, as it's the safest alternative to everyone involved.

MYTH 212. | *Skydivers can hear what each other are saying.* Due to the speed at which they're falling, no matter how loudly they yell at each other, they won't be able to hear anything.

MYTH 213. | *People can fit in ventilation shafts.*
While it's a popular method of sneaking around in
movies, a human being couldn't fit in most ventilation
shafts. Even if they could somehow climb into one,
ventilation shafts aren't designed to support an
average person's weight so they would quickly buckle
down.

MYTH 214. | *Suicide rates are highest during the
holidays.* In the United States, the highest suicide
rates are in April or May.

MYTH 215. | *Pencils have lead.* Pencils actually
have graphite inside of them and not lead.

MYTH 216. | *You can overdose on weed.*
Theoretically, it's possible if you were to smoke over
500 joints in a row. However, it's more likely that you
will overdose on coffee than on weed.

MYTH 217. | *Velcro is a substance.* Velcro is just a
brand name, and even the Velcro website will say that
Velcro, as a substance, doesn't exist.

MYTH 218. | *Teenagers are the most likely to
commit suicide.* In most countries, 50% of suicides
are committed by people that are over the age of 65.

MYTH 219. | *Prohibition made it illegal to drink
alcohol in the United States.* During Prohibition,
alcohol was illegal to be transported or sold but it
could be consumed.

MYTH 220. | *You get one phone call after you've been arrested.* All cells are equipped with a phone and you can make as many calls as you want as long as they are prepaid or collect calls.

MYTH 221. | *Galileo invented the telescope.* Hans Lippershey invented the telescope in 1608. However, Galileo found out about his inventions and made a much better version a few years later.

MYTH 222. | *A group of piranhas can eat any animal to bones in less than a minute.* Piranhas are actually scared of most animals, especially humans. They usually swim around until they find dead animals and eat them.

MYTH 223. | *Flamingos are pink because they eat shrimp.* Flamingos are pink because they eat blue-green algae.

MYTH 224. | *The first domesticated animal was the dog.* 14,000 years ago, the first animal to be domesticated was the reindeer by the Mongolians.

MYTH 225. | *Moths are attracted to fire because they think it's the Sun.* The reason why moths act strange near bright lights is because it makes them disoriented and not because they think it's the Sun.

MYTH 226. | *Polar bears are white.* A polar bear's fur is transparent and the white color that you see in their fur is actually snow.

MYTH 227. | *Polar bears and penguins live on the same Pole.* Actually, polar bears and penguins live on opposite Poles.

MYTH 228. | *Cats can drink milk.* Cats are lactose intolerant and it's extremely dangerous for them to drink milk.

MYTH 229. | *A blue whale can swallow a car.* While the blue whale is absolutely massive, it's throat is only big enough to swallow a beach ball.

MYTH 230. | *The longest animal is the blue whale.* The longest animal is the bootlace worm. The longest one ever found was over 180 feet long, which is nearly double the length of the blue whale.

MYTH 231. | *Humans are the only animals that experience menopause.* Killer whales also experience menopause.

MYTH 232. | *Killer whales are whales.* Killer whales are actually dolphins.

MYTH 233. | *Wolves howl at the moon.* Wolves howl to communicate with other wolves. The reason they do this at night is because they're nocturnal animals and they howl upwards because it helps them project the sound to farther distances.

MYTH 234. | *Sharks have to keep moving or they will die.* Sharks actually stop moving when they're sleeping. The ocean currents may move them around but they're not consciously moving themselves.

MYTH 235. | *Sharks kill more people than any other animal.* Sharks only kill about 5 people per year. The animal with the most kills is the hippo, which kills up to 3,000 people per year.

MYTH 236. | *Sharks can track you if you're bleeding in the ocean.* In fact, sharks can track you from just being in the water. Their senses are so tuned to the ocean that they can detect when something is interrupting the flow of the ocean current.

MYTH 237. | *Pigs are the dirties animals.* Pigs are one of the cleanest animals. They're one of the only farm animals that make sleeping arrangements in their pen. The reason why they're always covered in mud isn't because they're dirty, it's because they don't have sweat glands and the mud helps keep them cool.

MYTH 238. | *Peacocks use their tails to impress females.* The peacock doesn't use its tail to impress females but to intimidate predators.

MYTH 239. | *Mammoths went extinct in the Ice Age 15,000 years ago.* Mammoths went extinct 4,600 years ago. They were still around when the pyramids were being built.

MYTH 240. | *Jellyfish don't have eyes.* Box Jellyfish have 24 eyes. They're all evenly spread around its body and the jellyfish can move each one independently.

MYTH 241. | *Pigeons are infested with disease.* Despite being often compared to rats, there is little to no evidence that pigeons carry diseases.

MYTH 242. | *Only humans hold funerals for their dead.* Elephants bury their dead and mourn other elephants. It's even common for them to suffer from depression after the death of a loved one.

MYTH 243. | *Tigers are mostly found in the jungle.* There are twice as many tigers in the United States that in the rest of the world combined. However, a lot of the tigers were brought in through the illegal exotic wildlife trade.

MYTH 244. | *The lion is the king of the jungle.* The male lion is actually lazier and smaller than a tiger. Furthermore, lions live in Saharan Africa and Asia and not in the jungle.

MYTH 245. | *An octopus has eight legs.* The octopus has two legs and six arms. The octopus uses its six arms for eating while its two longer leg tentacles propel them forward.

MYTH 246. | *Hippos are slow.* Despite their massive size, a hippo can run up to 30 MPH.

MYTH 247. | *Centipedes are harmless.* Centipedes secrete cyanide, which is lethal at certain dosages.

MYTH 248. | *A platypus is harmless.* A platypus is venomous. When it's venom enters your body, it burns and can be deadly if not treated immediately by a medical professional.

MYTH 249. | *The musical instrument that a snake charmer uses can hypnotize a snake.* The snake is only responding to the movements of the snake charmer and not the instrument their playing. This means that the snake isn't under any hypnotic spell and might even bite the charmer if it gets bored.

MYTH 250. | *Black mamba snakes are black.* Black mambas get their name because the inside of their mouth is black.

MYTH 251. | *Mountain goats are goats.* A mountain goat is actually an antelope.

MYTH 252. | *Ostriches have the strongest kick in the animal kingdom.* The strongest kick in the animal kingdom comes from a zebra. A single kick exerts 15,000 Newtons of force, which is more than enough to kill a lion. To put things in perspective, Mike

Tyson in his prime could punch at around 3,500 Newtons.

MYTH 253. | *Apes only eat bananas.* While they do eat bananas, they eat a wide variety of other food, such as: berries, flowers, bark, stems and roots.

MYTH 254. | *Ostriches lay the largest eggs.* The whale shark lays the largest egg.

MYTH 255. | *Cockroaches would survive a nuclear holocaust.* While cockroaches can absorb at least 20,000 rads, which is 20 times more than us, it still wouldn't be able to survive a nuclear holocaust. A single nuclear explosion would expel 200,000 rads, which means that every single cockroach would be wiped along with us.

MYTH 256. | *Humans are the most adaptable animal on Earth.* While our intelligence plays a critical role to our survival, we still wouldn't be able to survive cataclysmic event. On the other hand, a tardigrade, a half-millimeter sized microorganism, can survive just about anything. If a tardigrade stops drinking water for a few minutes, it goes into a coma. Once in a coma, it's basically indestructible; it can be lit on fire, thrown in space, thrown in nuclear waste, have massive amounts of pressure applied to it and still survive. Then, if it's given even a drop of water, it would be awakened from its coma.

MYTH 257. | *Panthers exist.* Panthers aren't any specific animal. Any cat that can roar, such as tigers, lions and jaguars, are considered panthers.

MYTH 258. | *Dolly the sheep was the first cloned animal.* The first animal was cloned in 1885, well over a century before Dolly, and it was a sea urchin.

MYTH 259. | *Turkeys are originally from North America.* They actually originate from Mexico.

MYTH 260. | *Camels are the most common in the Middle East.* Australia has the most camels. In fact, they are so common in Australia that Saudi Arabia imports them from there.

MYTH 261. | *All oysters lay pearls.* The chance of an oyster laying a pearl is 1 in 1000.

MYTH 262. | *Chimpanzees have more hair than humans.* Chimpanzees have thicker hair than us but we have more hair follicles overall.

MYTH 263. | *Wolverines aren't real.* Wolverines are a small Canadian weasel that prefers to keep to itself. When cornered by a predator, it becomes vicious and attacks the predators neck almost instantly.

MYTH 264. | *Elephants can't jump.* An adult elephant can't jump but a young one can. The only mammals that can't jump at all are hippos and sloths.

MYTH 265. | *If you concentrate on doing sit-ups, you'll eventually have six-pack abs.* While sit-ups will make your abs stronger, they won't suddenly make you have abs. Abs are made in the kitchen and if you want to see your abs, then you'll have to lose the body fat to reveal them; this means having a healthy diet and a proper exercise regimen.

MYTH 266. | *The Big Bad Wolf from the Red Riding Hood book eats the grandmother.* In the earlier versions of the story, Red Riding Hood is the one who eats her own grandmother.

MYTH 267. | *Goldilocks was a young girl with blonde hair.* In the original folk tale, Goldilocks was an old woman with silver hair who broke her neck when she tried to run away from the bears.

MYTH 268. | *Mammals began evolving after the dinosaurs went extinct.* Mammals lived before, during and after the dinosaurs went extinct.

MYTH 269. | *All epileptics have seizures when exposed to flickering light.* Only 1 in 20 epileptics are photosensitive.

MYTH 270. | *Twins that are attached to each other are called Siamese Twins.* Twins that are attached to each other are called Conjoined Twins.

MYTH 271. | *The most common illness doctors deal with in the United States is the common cold.* Depression is the most common diagnosis in the United States. It's the fourth most common diagnosis worldwide, behind pneumonia, diarrhea, and AIDS.

MYTH 272. | *A psychopath is a serial killer.* Being a psychopath means the person can't experience human empathy. For example, when their friends are feeling depressed, they will feel happy and when their friends will feel happy, they will feel angry at their friends happiness. This doesn't mean that being a psychopath automatically means that the person will also be a serial killer.

MYTH 273. | *Only women can get breast cancer.* While women are a lot more likely to get breast cancer, men can get it as well.

MYTH 274. | *Nicotine causes cancer.* Nicotine creates the addiction to smoking, but it's the tar in cigarettes that causes cancer.

MYTH 275. | *Radiation from a cellphone can cause cancer.* The radiation that cellphones emit spread so wide and thin that it's almost harmless to humans.

MYTH 276. | *You can get the flu from a flu shot.* The flu shot contains a weakened version of the flu virus. This way, when the weakened version enters your body, your body can fight it off and create antibodies to fight it when the full version of the virus enters your body.

MYTH 277. | *Homosexual men are the most likely people to carry the AIDS virus.* The most common carriers of the AIDS virus are heterosexual women between the ages of 18-25.

MYTH 278. | *All deaf people use sign language.* Only 10% of deaf people use sign language.

MYTH 279. | *French fries originated in France.* French fries are actually Belgian and "frenching" means to cut into thin strips.

MYTH 280. | *Spaghetti originated in Italy.* Spaghetti originated in China. Magellan tasted it on his travels in Asian and brought it back to Venice, where it became popular.

MYTH 281. | *Apples originate from the United States.* Apples originate from Kazakhstan.

MYTH 282. | *Brazil nuts are nuts.* Brazil nuts are actually seeds.

MYTH 283. | *Peanuts are nuts.* Peanuts are actually beans.

MYTH 284. | *Coffee is made from beans.* Coffee comes from coffee seeds, not beans.

MYTH 285. | *Bananas grow on trees.* Bananas are berries that grow from a banana seed. In fact, it can be said that bananas grow on plants rather than trees.

MYTH 286. | *Decaffeinated coffee has no caffeine.* Decaffeinated coffee still has 3% caffeine.

MYTH 287. | *Coca-Cola was originally green.* Coca-Cola has always been brown in color, only the bottles were originally green.

MYTH 288. | *If you leave a tooth in Coca-Cola overnight, it will dissolve.* Coca-Cola will not dissolve a tooth overnight, but it will dissolve it eventually. This is because Coca-Cola contains phosphoric acid and citric acid, the same stuff found in orange juice; therefore, if you put a tooth in orange juice, it will also dissolve eventually.

MYTH 289. | *Honey has an expiry date.* Honey can last for over 32,000 years before going bad. By the time honey goes bad, you will be long gone.

MYTH 290. | *Ketchup is an American invention.* Ketchup was originally invented in China, 500 years ago. It was originally made from anchovies and not tomatoes.

MYTH 291. | *McDonalds is the world biggest food brand.* Subway is the biggest food brand in the world with 41,641 locations open worldwide, while McDonalds has 34,492 locations open worldwide.

MYTH 292. | *Carrots were always orange.* The carrots that we eat today have been heavily mutated over 5,000 years. Originally, carrots came from Afghanistan and they were purple with a yellow interior.

MYTH 293. | *If you drop your food, you can still eat it if it's spent less than five seconds on the floor.* Food is contaminated the second that it touches the ground.

MYTH 294. | *The first modern Olympic Games were set in Athens, Greece.* The first modern Olympic Games were set in Shropshire, England.

MYTH 295. | *The first Olympics used the discus.* The very first Olympics had only one event, and that was running.

MYTH 296. | *"Paralympics" is short for "Paraplegic Olympics".* "Paralympics" is actually short for "Parallel Olympics."

MYTH 297. | *Olympic Gold Medals are made out of gold.* 92.5% of all Olympic Gold Medals is silver, and the very small part left is gold.

MYTH 298. | *Football was invented in England.* Football originated in China and was the first known game in early 4 B.C. It was played almost exactly the same as we play it today.

MYTH 299. | *Baseball originated in the United States.* Baseball originated in England.

MYTH 300. | *The Egyptian Pyramids looked the same now as they did when they were originally built.* When the Pyramids were first built, they were covered in white limestone that would glow at night. Over time, weather and thieves took all of the white limestone, leaving the Pyramids looking as we know them today.

MYTH 301. | *When you're pregnant, you can't conceive another child.* While it is very rare, there are several documented instances of women getting pregnant once they're already pregnant. The event is called superfetation.

MYTH 302. | *You can't get a sunburn if you're under water.* Sunrays penetrate the water at up to 30 meters. In fact, people are more likely to get a sunburn while they're in the water because water absorbs sunlight.

MYTH 303. | *When you cut yourself, you should suck the wound.* While many people have done this, the mouth is one of the worst places to put your open wound in. The mouth is filled with bacteria and you're much more likely to get your wound infected.

MYTH 304. | *You can get an STD from a toilet seat.* Any STD that has been exposed to air would die within minutes, therefore, severely limiting any chance of a person contracting an STD from a toilet seat.

MYTH 305. | *Whitening your teeth is healthy.* The procedure that whitens your teeth actually damages the enamel. If you get your teeth whitened, they will appear healthier, but will be far more damaged in the long run.

MYTH 306. | *Leaning your neck back when you have a nosebleed.* Leaning back when you have a nose bleed causes the blood to go into your throat, which can make you sick. Leaning forward lessens the bleeding and clears your nose.

MYTH 307. | *Contact lenses can get stuck behind your eye.* There is no cavity behind your eye, therefore, the lens would have nowhere to go.

MYTH 308. | *Injecting someone directly in the heart is possible.* Doctors will never inject a syringe directly into the heart as it would tear open the heart tissue and kill the person.

MYTH 309. | *You can only get chickenpox once.* You can actually get chickenpox as an adult as well, even if you've had them as a child. However, as an adult, getting chickenpox would also mean that you're very likely to get shingles as well.

MYTH 310. | *Humans have two nostrils.* We actually have four nostrils, two external ones that we can see and two internal ones, called choannae, that are connected to the inside of your throat.

MYTH 311. | *A woman doesn't have an Adam's apple.* All women have Adam's apples, they're just not as pronounced as a mans.

MYTH 312. | *Your fingers have muscles.* There are no muscles in your fingers, all finger movements are done by the muscles in the forearm and palm.

MYTH 313. | *Humans are born with 200 bones.* Humans are born with 300 bones but, by the age of six, bones ossify to form 206 bones.

MYTH 314. | *Washing your hands with hot water kills the most germs.* You would have to be washing your hands with water that is at least 80 degrees Celsius to kill the germs on your hands, which simply isn't realistic. Even intense scrubbing under water with soap doesn't kill germs, it simply removes them from your hand so you can wash them down the drain.

MYTH 315. | *Reading a book in dim light will damage you eyes.* When reading in a dim light, the muscles around the pupils contract so that they can let in more light. This can strain your eyes but it won't damage your eyesight.

MYTH 316. | *Some people don't have dreams when they sleep.* Everyone has dreams, some people just don't remember theirs. In fact, the average person has about nine dreams every single night.

MYTH 317. | *Cleaning your ears with cotton buds is good for your ears.* Actually, earwax is there to protect your ears. Pushing a cotton bud into your ear will push the earwax further down your ear, which makes you far more prone to infections.

MYTH 318. | *Washing your hair every day is healthy.* Your hair produces natural oils that will preserve your hair for longer. By shampooing it every single day, you don't allow your hair the chance to absorb the oil.

MYTH 319. | *Doing crossword puzzles will keep your brain mentally alert.* While doing crossword puzzles may improve your ability to find words, they won't help your brain's overall cognition or memory.

MYTH 320. | *A person's personality displays a right brain or left brain dominance.* The two sides of the brain are fully co-dependent on each other. Brain scanning technology has found that the two hemispheres of the brain work together in complex processing. For example, language processing, which was always believed to be handled by the left side of the brain, is now understood to take place in both parts; the left side processes grammar while the right processes intonation.

MYTH 321. | *Brain damage is always permanent.* The brain can repair and compensate for certain injuries, and even generate brand new cells to help it recover. Recently, researchers have found that the brain remains plastic throughout its life and can rewire itself very quickly in response to learning.

MYTH 322. | *Drinking alcohol kills brain cells.* Moderate alcohol use won't destroy any of your brain cells, but constant alcohol use can damage the brain, not the cells. Alcoholics often experience brain damage due to the alcohol damaging the dendrites that are found at the end of the neurons in your brain, not by killing off brain cells.

MYTH 323. | *You must speak one language before learning another.* Children who learn English can also learn French at the same time, without confusing one language with the other. While some people believe that learning one language would interfere with learning another at the same time, young children who learn two language at the same time, gain better generalized knowledge of language structure as a whole.

MYTH 324. | *The bigger the brain, the smarter the person.* This myth can easily be busted by looking at different animal species. An average whale's brain can weigh up to 20 pounds, while an average humans brain can weigh up to 3 pounds. Knowing that we are more intelligent than whales, it clearly shows that a bigger brain doesn't necessarily mean a smarter being.

MYTH 325. | *Drugs create holes in the brain.*
Physical trauma is the only way a hole can be created
in a brain. While drugs affect the function of the
brain's neurotransmitters, they can't make a physical
hole in your brain.

MYTH 326. | *The human body can "sweat out"*
toxins. Sweat glands are found in your skin, and since
they're not connected to any other part of your body's
systems, they can't eliminate toxins. Sweat is the
body's way of cooling itself, not a way for the body to
release toxins.

MYTH 327. | *You should starve yourself when you*
have a fever and feed yourself when you have a cold.
Having plenty of fluids and energy is key to
overcoming a fever or a cold. Not eating would
simply put your body in a state of starvation and
make it even harder to get better.

MYTH 328. | *Milk increases the mucus in your nose*
when you're sick. While milk does temporarily
thicken mucus, it doesn't actually produce more
mucus.

MYTH 329. | *Blood in your veins is blue.* The blood
in your veins isn't blue, it just looks that way because
of the light being diffused by your skin. Blood
changes color based on how much oxygen is in it; it
can go from bright red when its oxygenated to dark
red when it's not.

MYTH 330. | *Humans can become resistant to certain antibiotics.* Humans can't become resistant to antibiotics but bacteria can. If you take a certain medication many times over a long course of time, there is a chance that the bacteria in your body can become accustomed and immune to it.

MYTH 331. | *Chocolate and fried foods cause acne.* Acne is caused by many different things, like cosmetics, sweating, high humidity, genetics, bacteria, etc. However, eating chocolate or fried foods won't cause you to suddenly get acne.

MYTH 332. | *Coffee will sober you up.* You become sober once the alcohol has been processed through your system, and coffee won't speed up the process. However, caffeine can trick your brain into thinking you're sober, when you're really not.

MYTH 333. | *Cancer is a single disease.* Cancer is a term for over 200 diseases that all behave in a similar way. However, all of them require different forms of treatment, so there can never be just one cure for cancer.

MYTH 334. | *When you sneeze, your heart stops for a second.* Sneezing is a reflex that's sent from your brain when something tickles the upper lining of your nose. What happens is that the nerves send a signal to your brain which makes you sneeze. However, this doesn't stop your heart.

MYTH 335. | *Cold showers can help sober people up.* Drinking alcohol lowers the bodies core body temperature, and a cold shower would simply put the person at risk for hypothermia. The only thing that can sober a person up is time and rest.

MYTH 336. | *Heart attacks hurt.* Heart attacks will rarely hurt and 60% of them go completely unnoticed. If they do hurt, it usually comes in the form of a heartburn, tooth ache or just a strange feeling in your chest. Some heart attacks can even last hours before any symptoms arise; those are usually the most fatal.

MYTH 337. | *If you've swallowed poison, you should vomit.* Most poisons are acidic or alkaline and since your stomach produces its own acid, it might be able to deal with it better than your throat or lungs would after you try to vomit.

MYTH 338. | *Organic food is more nutritious.* What makes a difference in nutrients is how long a certain product sits on the shelf at a grocery store and not if its organic or not. For example, spinach loses about half of its foliate within a week.

MYTH 339. | *Organic food tastes better.* Multiple studies have done blind taste tests on organic and non-organic food. They found that people can't tell the difference if the food is organic or not. The only difference people can taste is if the food has been produced locally or if its imported, since imported food tends to have spent a long time in transit, thus giving it a staler taste.

MYTH 340. | *You don't have to be careful about washing organic food.* All products, no matter if they're organic or not, are susceptible to bacteria. Everything that's bought at a store or grown in your own backyard should be washed thoroughly under water.

MYTH 341. | *Organic food is better for you.* Organic food has the same nutritional value as non-organic food. Therefore, if you're eating organic chips, it's just as bad for you as if you've been eating regular chips.

MYTH 342. | *Canola oil is not good for human consumption.* Extensive studies have been done on animals and humans by nutritional scientists, in which they've concluded that canola oil is safe for human consumption. In fact, it is recommended by the National Heart Foundation due to its benefits relating to heart disease.

MYTH 343. | *Skipping breakfast can help you lose weight.* Research has shown that people who skip breakfast tend to have higher body weights than those who regularly eat breakfast. This is because the people who skip breakfast tend to snack on unhealthy alternatives during the day.

MYTH 344. | *All fats are bad for you.* Fats are essential for good health and they do protect us from various cancers and heart disease. There are two types of healthy fats, monounsaturated and polyunsaturated fat, found in nuts, seeds, fish, etc. In fact, a healthy diet must include a good amount of fat.

MYTH 345. | *Avoiding carbohydrates after 5 PM will help you lose weight.* There were studies done that show that the body doesn't react any differently if you were to eat carbohydrates after 5 PM. This is simply a method that people use to help them lose weight by decreasing overall calories they consume.

MYTH 346. | *Fresh vegetables are more nutritious than frozen vegetables.* Since frozen vegetables tend to be picked in their prime and flash-frozen right after harvesting, they tend to retain more nutrients than fresh vegetables.

MYTH 347. | *A cleanse or detox is good for you.* Your body already cleanses you as part of its daily function. You don't need to buy any teas or pills to accomplish that.

MYTH 348. | *Low carbohydrate diets are good for you.* Your brain needs carbohydrates to function. Your body can't tell which types of carbohydrates you feed it, so it's best to get them from whole grains and fruits, as those foods are packed with other types of nutrients as well.

MYTH 349. | *Apples are as good for you now as they always were.* While apples are a good source of essential nutrients, an apple that was grown in 1940 contained 3 times as much iron as an apple grown today. This is because the continuous growing of the same crop in the same soil removes the nutrients from the fruit.

MYTH 350. | *Radiation from a mobile phone is strong enough to cook an egg in 10 minutes.* When placed between two active mobile phones, if you leave an egg for 24 hours, it will not even warm up by one tenth of a degree.

MYTH 351. | *Artificial sweeteners help you lose weight.* A study on rats at Purdue University in Indiana, found that artificial sweeteners break down the link between sweet tastes and calories, which gives you the feeling of hunger, even if you're full.

MYTH 352. | *Chocolate is an antidepressant.* Chocolate was claimed to have the ability to boost serotonin levels, which make you feel good. Serotonin levels increase only if the protein content of the food is less than 2% and chocolate contains about 5% of protein.

MYTH 353. | *Vodka has no calories.* Vodka doesn't have any carbohydrates but a single 30 milliliter shot has 103.5 calories.

MYTH 354. | *Red wine is good for your heart.* University of Texas researchers found that, although moderate drinkers lived longer than those who didn't drink at all, wine drinkers weren't any better than those that drank beer or spirits.

MYTH 355. | *Brown eggs are healthier than white eggs.* Though they tend to cost 20% more than white eggs, it's all the same egg. The only difference between the two is that they come from a different breed of hen.

MYTH 356. | *Sea salt has less sodium than table salt.* Both salts have about the same amount of sodium per teaspoon, which is 2,300 milligrams.

MYTH 357. | *Celery has negative calories.* While celery is very low in calories, there are no foods that have negative calories, which means that you burn more calories digesting the food than you do eating it.

MYTH 358. | *It takes 21 days to form a new habit.* A study done on evaluated behavior change found that creating a new habit takes an average of 66 days. However, the study also found that there were wide variations between its subjects; for example, some would take 18 days while others would take 254 days.

MYTH 359. | *Muscle can turn to fat.* Many people believe that when you stop exercising, your muscle will turn into fat. What really happens, however, is that when you stop exercising, your muscle mass declines, which means that your body burns less calories. However, you still eat just as many calories as when you had the muscle, therefore, the increase in calories causes you to put on weight.

MYTH 360. | *Some people can eat whatever they want and still lose weight.* To lose weight you have to lose more calories than you intake. Some people may seem to get away with eating any kind of food but, what people don't see, is that those people use more energy for their daily tasks, therefore, burning through their food and drink intake.

MYTH 361. | *Skipping meals is a good way to lose weight.* Skipping meals will often lead to overeating for your next meal, which would make you gain weight.

MYTH 362. | *Lifting weights isn't a good way to lose weight because it'll make you appear "bulky".* Lifting weights builds strong muscles, which is an excellent base for someone to start on their weight loss journey. Additionally, a body that has more muscle will burn more calories for just getting up in the morning and going about their day.

MYTH 363. | *Eating meat is bad for your health.* Lean meat is a necessity in a healthy diet. While chicken, fish, and red meat do contain some cholesterol, they also contain lots of iron, protein and zinc.

MYTH 364. | *Everyone should eat a gluten free diet.* Unless you have celiac disease, there's no reason to avoid them. Studies done on gluten free diets have found no lasting benefits of the diet to people who don't have celiac disease.

MYTH 365. | *Superfoods will keep you healthy.* "Superfoods" is just a marketing gimmick and there's no type of food that is packed with every single nutrient. Expensive foods like acai berries are marketed as being "superfoods" but basic foods like blueberries and apples have just as many antioxidants and vitamins in them as acai berries.

MYTH 366. | *Eating too much sugar gives you diabetes.* Eating too much sugar places you at risk for gaining too much weight. Being overweight is what puts you at risk for Type 2 Diabetes.

MYTH 367. | *Washing raw meat before cooking gets rid of bacteria.* This is a common myth but the fact is that when you cook the meat, the heat alone will kill all the bacteria that was living in the meat.

MYTH 368. | *All preservatives are bad for your health.* Preservatives are added to food in order to extend its shelf life and prevent bacterial growth. It's an absolute necessity for food to have preservatives so they can last the transportation and shelf life of a product in a grocery store. While some people can be sensitive to certain preservatives, preservatives have been used for centuries without any negative health effects.

MYTH 369. | *A high protein diet is bad for your bones and kidneys.* A high protein diet actually improves bone health and lowers the risk of bone fracture. In addition, studies have shown that high protein diets help with kidney disease and lower the risk of diabetes and high blood pressure.

MYTH 370. | *The Fourth of July is when America first declared independence from the British Empire.* It was on July 2nd when the Continental Congress voted for independence. Two day later, a revised version of the Declaration of Independence came about.

MYTH 371. | *The Pilgrims escaped religious intolerance in Europe to establish freedom in the New World.* The Pilgrims were frustrated with the Church of England so they first left for Amsterdam. Once there, they feared that their children would become too Dutch so they left to America. In America, non-puritans were outlawed from the colonies and had their voting rights taken away. It wasn't until the founding fathers separated church and state that religious freedom took effect.

MYTH 372. | *The Texans stationed at the Alamo in 1836 died fighting for their rights.* The Texans died fighting for their right to maintain the slave trade.

MYTH 373. | *Paul Revere rode through the night to warn the colonists that, "the British are coming!"* What really happened is that Revere rode in silence to avoid army patrols while spreading the word to key people. He also used the warning, "the regulars are coming out," as opposed to "the British" since many colonists were still loyal to the crown.

MYTH 374. | *The Wild West was extremely violent.* This myth is wildly exaggerated. For example, bank robberies took place only 12 times on the frontier from 1859 to 1900 and the average number of frontier town murders was 1.5 per year.

MYTH 375. | *The United States brought about the end of World War II.* It was actually the USSR that brought about the end as Hitler began an invasion of the USSR in 1941 and lost over 80% of Germany's force, along with massive amounts of war supplies and materials.

MYTH 376. | *Jewish slaves built the pyramids.* Recent archaeological finds show that Egyptians built the pyramids themselves. The pharaohs had only the finest craftsmen work on their pyramids because of the importance that they held for them.

MYTH 377. | *Cleopatra was Egyptian.* Cleopatra belonged to the Ptolemaic dynasty, a family of Greek origin that ruled Egypt after Alexander the Great.

MYTH 378. | *A cow kicking over a lantern caused the Great Chicago Fire.* The fire actually started in a small alley for unknown reasons. The journalist who attributed the fire to the cow kicking over a lit lantern, admitted he made the story up.

MYTH 379. | *Wall Street traders jumped to their deaths during the market crash of 1929.* Between Black Thursday and the end of 1929, only 4 suicides were linked to the events that began the Great Depression. Of those 4 suicides, only 2 happened on Wall Street.

MYTH 380. | *Iron maidens were invented during the Medieval period.* Iron maidens were made in the 18th century and were pieced together from artifacts in museums in order to attract more visitors. They weren't even used for torture.

MYTH 381. | *Cinco de Mayo is Mexico's Independence Day.* Cinco de Mayo isn't Mexico's Independence Day, it celebrates their victory against the French in the Battle of Puebla.

MYTH 382. | *In Rome, vomitoriums were used for vomiting.* Vomitoriums weren't used for vomiting, they were actually the entrances and exists for the stadiums.

MYTH 383. | *Sharks are never full.* Sharks actually only eat one seal pup every three days.

MYTH 384. | *Fire and lava only burn if they touch you.* You can actually get flash burns from standing close to lava, that's why volcanologists wear suits.

MYTH 385. | *Rudolph the Red-Nosed Reindeer was male.* Rudolph was actually a female because it had antlers. Male reindeer lose their antlers in winter.

MYTH 386. | *When you listen to a seashell, you can hear the ocean.* The sound that you hear from the seashell is just air resonating in a hollowed object. You can hear the same effect if you put a cup to your ear.

MYTH 387. | *Sardines are a type of fish.* A tin of sardines is just many types of fish put together, with each tin varying in the types of fish used.

MYTH 388. | *Polar bears are dying out due to the melting ice caps.* Actually, polar bears have been spotted in areas with melted snow, but people fail to recognize them as their fur turns brown.

MYTH 389. | *Cats stroke you because they like you.* Cats don't see themselves as pets, rather, they see themselves as the master and you as the pet. Humans feed them, stroke them, buy things for them, so the cat stroke reminds you that you are its property.

MYTH 390. | *Cats present their prey to you as a gift.* Cats present their prey to you because they are trying to show you how to catch prey. They don't understand how humans acquire food, believing that you need to hunt for what you will eat.

MYTH 391. | *Manual transmission in cars give better fuel economy than automatics.* Recent advances in technology, such as continuously variable transmission, eliminates the advantage of manuals.

MYTH 392. | *You can make your car more powerful by filling it with jet fuel.* Conventional car engines can't combust kerosene, which is jet fuel.

MYTH 393. | *Turning on the air conditioner is better for fuel economy than opening the window.* A 2004 study done by GM and SAE found that, for both sedans and SUVs, at a variety of speeds, turning the A/C on uses more fuel than driving with the windows down.

MYTH 394. | *Using your cell phone while filing up your gas can cause an explosion.* The Federal Communications Commission investigated this myth and found that there are no documented incidents where the use of a mobile phone caused a fire or an explosion at a gas station.

MYTH 395. | *Gas is cheaper in the morning.* The logic behind this myth is that, since temperatures are cooler in the morning, gasoline is denser and you can get more fuel per gallon pumped. However, the Consumer Report explained that gasoline is stored in underground tanks, where the temperature hardly fluctuates.

MYTH 396. | *Off-brand gas will hurt your car.* Off-brand gas has to meet the same standards as any brand name gasoline. The only difference might be that Mobil and Shell claim that they put extra engine-cleaning additives in their gasoline.

MYTH 397. | *Electric cars are more likely to catch on fire after a crash.* In 2012, the National Highway Traffic Safety Administration investigated this claim and found that no electric vehicles pose a greater risk of fire than gasoline-powered vehicle.

MYTH 398. | *A dirty car is more fuel efficient than a clean one.* Dirty particles actually create more drag and can reduce the fuel economy by 10%.

MYTH 399. | *Premium gas makes a non-premium car run better.* Premium gas makes a difference in powerful engines, but no difference on average cars.

MYTH 400. | *Red cars are pulled over for speeding more often than other cars.* A study by Quality Planning found that the most-ticketed car in 2013 was the grey Mercedes Benz SL convertible. This means that, when it comes to being pulled over, color doesn't make any difference.

MYTH 401. | *Charles Darwin was not well known before his work, "On the Origin of Species."* Darwin was actually well known and well respected in the scientific community before his work came out. His peers even described him as an "accomplished naturalist."

MYTH 402. | *Charles Darwin was the first to publish a book on evolution.* The idea of evolution dated back to the 7th century BC. In the early 19th century, there was even a theory of evolution proposed by a Catholic scientist named Jean-Baptise Lamarck.

MYTH 403. | *Scientists around the world dismissed Darwin's theories.* While some didn't agree at first, many did agree and even praised Darwin and his findings. A statement in Wilberforce even said, "a beautiful illustration of the wonderful interdependence of nature-of the golden chain of unsuspected relations which bind together all the mighty web which stretches from end to end of this full and most diversified Earth."

MYTH 404. | *Charles Darwin coined the term "survival of the fittest."* It was Herbert Spencer who coined the phrase, "survival of the fittest," when he read Darwin's work on evolution.

MYTH 405. | *Charles Darwin was an atheist.* He was confronted with such allegations even when he was alive, and he denied all of them in correspondence, letters and in his own autobiography. He said, "I have never been an atheist in the sense of denying the existence of a God."

MYTH 406. | *Subliminal advertising works.* Many studies have been done on this topic through carefully controlled laboratory trials and the researchers found that subliminal messages didn't affect the subjects consumer choices or voting preferences.

MYTH 407. | *There's an autism epidemic.* While the number of cases of autism from the 1990s to now have increased suddenly, the reason isn't because there is an epidemic it's because the diagnostic criteria for autism have been significantly loosened. However, when a 2005 study conducted in England tracked autism cases between 1992 and 1998 using the diagnostic criteria from the early 1990s, they found that the rates didn't change.

MYTH 408. | *Opposites attract.* Though it's widely believed that people are attracted to those who are different than them, recent studies have shown that that's not the case; people prefer to be with people who share similar views and interests.

MYTH 409. | *Dreams have symbolic meaning.* Dreaming is just a random representation of your brain's actions when it tries to sort together information and experience that you have given it. It works a lot like a filing system, shifting through all the memories you've created and organizing them in different places.

MYTH 410. | *Our memory works like a recorder.*
Memory isn't reproductive, meaning it duplicates
exactly what we experience, but reconstructive, which
means that we remember a blurry mixture of what
actually happened, along with our beliefs, needs,
emotions and hunches mixed in.

MYTH 411. | *Playing Mozart to your baby will
make it more likely to become a genius.* Recent
studies have found that playing Mozart to your baby
has no outside effects other than helping the baby
keep calm.

MYTH 412. | *You need 8 hours of sleep every night.*
The amount of sleep a person need varies from 5
hours to 8 hours; however, an average person needs,
at most, 7 hours of sleep.

MYTH 413. | *Humid air is heavier than dry air.* Dry
air is heavier than humid air. There are more
molecules of water in humid air which are lighter
than molecules of air. While you can feel the presence
of humid air, it's a lot less dense than dry air.

MYTH 414. | *Tornadoes don't strike cities or
mountainous areas.* The presence of rough terrain or
skyscrapers can disrupt and weaken a tornado, but
that doesn't mean that tornadoes wouldn't happen.
Tornadoes have touched down in Texas and other
Midwestern cities and have hit skyscrapers.

MYTH 415. | *It's safe to drive through flood water.* It only takes 2 feet of moving water to lift a car off the road. More than half of all flash flood related deaths are because people thought that they can drive through flood water.

MYTH 416. | *All probiotic supplements are the same.* Almost every single probiotic supplement is different because they all differ in how many strains of organisms they have in their mixture. Also, each strain can have different species living in them.

MYTH 417. | *The United States is going bankrupt.* Unlike a business or a household, the United States government has the ability to tax, print money and borrow funds at a rate given by the central bank. It's also supported by a unified federal government, central treasury, and a central bank. Therefore, no, the United States will not go bankrupt.

MYTH 418. | *The free market can solve all problems.* Capitalism, when left by itself, will pursue profit maximization and nothing else. This will naturally turn into monopolies and unregulated monopolies mean small wages, little employment, consumer loss, and increased inequality.

MYTH 419. | *Everybody has allergies.* Only about 1 in 5 people in the United States have allergies. While there is a rise in seasonal and food allergies over the past 20 years, it still doesn't mean that "everybody" has them.

MYTH 420. | *You can't develop seasonal allergies as an adult.* The body can become highly allergic to new things all the time. If you didn't have allergies when you were younger, there's a chance you'll have them when you're older just like if you had allergies when you were a child, there's a chance that they will go away when you're older.

MYTH 421. | *Scientists can predict a bad pollen season.* Only when forecasters can predict a number of dry days in a row without rain, like when there's a severe drought, can scientists make any prediction on pollen.

MYTH 422. | *Flowers are a common trigger for seasonal allergies.* Flower pollens are pretty heavy and fall to the ground, rather than linger in air. Tree pollens and pollen from grasses and weeds is very light and is likely to stay airborne and cause allergies to flare up.

MYTH 423. | *Private browsing online keeps you anonymous.* If you're using Incognito Mode on Google Chrome, it just means that the browser won't keep track of your history, import your bookmarks, or automatically log you into any of your accounts.

MYTH 424. | *Leaving your phone plugged into the charger, damages the battery.* Many people believe that leaving your phone to charge overnight damages the battery, however, there's nothing to back this claim up. Modern smartphones run on lithium ion batteries, which are advanced enough to know when to stop charging once capacity is reached.

MYTH 425. | *More megapixels means a better camera.* The quality of an image is determined by how much light the sensor can take in. Typically, bigger sensors come with bigger pixels, but the pixels tend to be larger as well. In the end, it's the size of the megapixels that matters more than how many of them there are.

MYTH 426. | *Higher resolution is always better.* The human eye can't discern the very fine detail when a display packs more than 300 pixels per inch. After a certain point, the resolution really doesn't matter as the eye can't even see the detail.

MYTH 427. | *It's bad to use your iPad charger for your iPhone.* While it could stress the battery slightly, it would take a year or more to notice any changes in the batteries efficiency.

MYTH 428. | *You shouldn't turn your computer off every day.* Shutting it down actually places less stress on its components, since they don't have to be working all the time, which enables it to last longer.

MYTH 429. | *Breastfeeding makes your child smarter.* Breastfeeding won't make your child smarter. Intelligence is linked closely to the genetics the parents pass down to the child and the child's willingness to learn.

MYTH 430. | *Breastfeeding doesn't protect your baby against infections.* Breastfeeding does protect your baby from infections when they're young. There have been reports that breastfeeding helps protect babies from diarrhea and chest infections.

MYTH 431. | *If you take birth control, you won't get HIV.* Birth control only prevents pregnancy, not HIV. Condoms are the only contraceptive that prevents pregnancies and some STDs, like HIV.

MYTH 432. | *You can get HIV from kissing someone who is infected.* HIV transmission can only happen by having unprotected sex or by sharing needles with someone who is infected. There has never been a documented case of infection from saliva.

MYTH 433. | *It's fine to have unprotected sex if you and your partner are both HIV positive.* HIV supreinfection can take place, in which, a second strain of HIV infects both people. The second strain can evolve differently in the person's body, making it a lot more difficult to treat.

MYTH 434. | *Snakes have one penis.* Snakes actually have two penises. Each penis is called a hemipenis, or "half penis".

MYTH 435. | *Urinating on an electric fence can't cause electrocution.* Urinating on an electric fence can cause electrocution because electricity can travel up the urine stream and into the body.

MYTH 436. | *Marilyn Manson had his ribs removed so he could give himself a blow job.* Manson is a completely average person when he's not onstage. The persona that he created is purely meant for his music career and in no way reflects who he is. Therefore, Manson did not remove his ribs so he could give himself a blow job.

MYTH 437. | *Marilyn Manson played Paul Pfeiffer on The Wonder Years.* Even though they look alike, Paul Saviano was the actor who played Paul Pfeiffer on The Wonder Years.

MYTH 438. | *Lauryn Hill would rather die than have a white person buy her albums.* Hill publicly stated that she doesn't hate white people, but that she loves black people and makes music for them.

MYTH 439. | *Jack White and Meg White are brother and sister.* In early interviews, Jack White told reporters that they were siblings. However, they were actually married and divorced, with Jack White taking Meg's name and keeping it after the divorce.

MYTH 440. | *Ciara was born with a penis.* The myth started in the early 2000s and followed the artist throughout her career. However, it's not true, Ciara was born a female.

MYTH 441. | *Courtney Love killed Kurt Cobain.* Kurt Cobain committed suicide. He struggled his entire life with bipolar disorder and drug addiction.

MYTH 442. | *Rihanna slept with Jay-Z when she was 17 to jump start her career.* This has been a long standing rumor but Rihanna was launched into her career with her single "SOS" going platinum and topping Billboard Hot 100 charts for three weeks.

MYTH 443. | *Lady Gaga is a hermaphrodite.* A hermaphrodite is a person with both sex organs and in 2009, Lady Gaga publicly stated that she was actually just a woman.

MYTH 444. | *A person can have the Ebola virus and be contagious without knowing it.* According to the World Health Organization, an Ebola patient is only contagious when they are showing symptoms.

MYTH 445. | *You can catch Ebola if someone coughs or sneezes on you.* Ebola isn't airborne, meaning that you can't catch it from people coughing and sneezing. It's spread through a person's broken skin or mucous membranes coming into contact with bodily fluids of infected people.

MYTH 446. | *The average penis size is 8 inches.*
According to the National Health Service, the average
size of an erect penis is about 6 inches.

MYTH 447. | *Certain foods work as aphrodisiacs.*
Foods that boost your overall energy might increase
your libido in the long run, but it would be indirectly.
Healthy food that makes you feel more energetic will
make you happier, and the happier you are, the better
your libido will be.

MYTH 448. | *Watching porn rewires your brain.*
While it does to some degree, it's not permanent.
People who have porn addictions don't have it
because of porn itself, but because they have
addictive personalities. Porn is part of our culture and
many people watch it without experiencing any kind
of side effects.

MYTH 449. | *Women are naturally more bisexual
than men.* In Britain, 1% of men and 1.4% of women
aged 16 to 74 identify themselves as bisexual.
Judging from this statistic, there is really no
significant gender difference between men and
women who identify as bisexual.

MYTH 450. | *Most people have sex before the age
of 16.* Only around 30% of people have sex before the
age of 16, and this statistic hasn't changed in the last
decade.

MYTH 451. | *You can tell how big a man's penis is by looking at his feet.* A study in 1993 on the relationship among height, penis length and foot size found that the correlation between penis length and height and shoe size was so weak that it couldn't be used as any type of predictor.

MYTH 452. | *The vaccine will completely shield you from getting the flu.* While a vaccine does help, there are so many different flu viruses that the vaccine can't possibly protect you from all of them.

MYTH 453. | *Zinc cures colds.* A study done in 2014 found that zinc can make colds last shorter, but the effect was so small that it doesn't make any difference in general.

MYTH 454. | *Vegetarians don't get enough protein.* There are plenty of beans and nuts that are high in protein and that vegetarians can eat. Also, it's important to note that the average woman needs only 46g of protein per day and an average man needs about 56g.

MYTH 455. | *You shouldn't exercise when you're pregnant.* It's perfectly healthy and recommended for pregnant women to get regular exercise throughout their pregnancies.

MYTH 456. | *You can't get pregnant if you are on your period.* While it's rare, you actually can get pregnant while you're on your period. Sperm can live inside your system for up to 7 days.

MYTH 457. | *Putting batteries in the fridge will help extend their life.* The condensation in the fridge can cause corrosion that will decrease the shelf life of your batteries.

MYTH 458. | *Toothpaste only works if it's foaming.* The foam is just a side effect of sodium lauryl sulfate, a synthetic detergent, that can cause negative effects like hypersensitivity.

MYTH 459. | *If food isn't consumed by its expiry date, it will go bad.* The expiry date just reflects when the product can no longer be guaranteed to be at peak quality, but you can still eat it without getting any side effects.

MYTH 460. | *Double dipping your chips into salsa spreads germs.* In laboratory tests, the difference in the amount of germs present after double dipping when compared to a single dip, is completely negligible.

MYTH 461. | *The best way to remove ink stains from your clothes is with hairspray.* It's actually the alcohol that's in the hairspray that can help with removing the stains.

MYTH 462. | *You need to use wood polish every time you clean wooden furniture.* Wood polish can contain oils that attract even more dust and if you use it often, the polish can dull the wood.

MYTH 463. | *There's a lot of genetic difference between each race.* A study in 2002 that dealt with genetics, found that there are bigger differences between Africans than there are between Africans and Eurasians.

MYTH 464. | *Modern humans didn't evolve in Africa.* Early homosapiens evolved into modern humans in Africa around 200,000 years ago. After, they migrated into different parts of the world in a span of 60,000 years.

MYTH 465. | *Neanderthals were not intelligent.* Neanderthals had advanced tools and were skilled hunters and socializers. While scientists are still not sure why exactly they went extinct, the theory is a lot more complicated than homosapiens outsmarting them and killing them off.

MYTH 466. | *Neanderthals didn't exist at the same time as humans.* At first, scientists thought that Neanderthals evolved into humans over time. However, when archaeologists found and dated human skeletons, they found that humans and Neanderthals co-existed for thousands of years.

MYTH 467. | *Neanderthals did not have sex with humans.* A team of researchers looked at Neanderthal genome in 2010 and if it was present in modern humans. They found that most humans living outside of Africa have about 1-4% of Neanderthal DNA in them.

MYTH 468. | *Earth is the only place where water exists.* There is a lot of evidence that Mars had a lot of water, along with other planets and moons in our solar system. Just this year alone, researchers found oceans on Jupiter's largest moon, Ganymede.

MYTH 469. | *Complex organisms like humans have more genes than simple organisms like an amoeba.* Humans actually have around 19,000 to 20,000 genes, while a moss plant has around 32,000 genes.

MYTH 470. | *King Tut was murdered.* A 2014 virtual autopsy on King Tut's body found that he died due to being ridden with diseases and deformations due to inbreeding.

MYTH 471. | *The universe is slowing down.* In the 1990s, scientists thought that gravity must be slowing down the expansion of the universe. However, recent studies have shown that the universe is expanding at an even faster rate.

MYTH 472. | *Birds don't have any intelligence.* A 2005 study found that some birds, such as parrots and crows, have almost ape-like intelligence.

MYTH 473. | *The universe is 13.73 billion years old.* The European Space Agency's Planck mission found that the universe is 13.82 billion years old.

MYTH 474. | *Gun ownership in the United States is increasing.* Though the gun sales are increasing, the portion of the population that owns guns is decreasing.

MYTH 475. | *Being in the military increases the likelihood of suicide.* The military is made up of a male heavy demographic that is more susceptible to suicide. If you control a few factors like age, sex and race, the military has a lower suicide rate than the rest of the country.

MYTH 476. | *1 in 10 Americans have a passport.* The actual figure is 37%.

MYTH 477. | *Crocodiles are slow on land.* Crocodiles can move up to 10 MPH on land.

MYTH 478. | *Penguins tip over when they look up towards planes flying above.* While penguins can get scared and flee to their nests, they can keep their footing when they're looking up.

MYTH 479. | *Goldfish are weak.* Goldfish can survive for hours outside of water. They do this by going into some sort of hibernation until they're returned to the water.

MYTH 480. | *There are three states of mater.* Actually, there are four: solid, liquid, gas and plasma.

MYTH 481. | *Black holes are black.* The only reason black holes appear black is because they suck in all the light.

MYTH 482. | *The center of the planet is molten.* The center of the planet is actually an extremely dense sphere of iron and nickel.

MYTH 483. | *Mercury is the hottest planet.* Even though Mercury is the closest planet to the Sun, Venus is the hottest planet. It has an average surface temperature of 864 degrees Fahrenheit or 462 degrees Celsius.

MYTH 484. | *Roasted chicken is healthier than fried chicken.* Just one chicken leg from a roasted chicken contains the same amount of fat as a scoop of ice cream; therefore, the roasted chicken is just about as healthy as fried chicken.

MYTH 485. | *Coconut milk is healthy.* Just a quarter of a can of coconut milk is three quarters of your daily recommended intake of saturated fats.

MYTH 486. | *Carrot cake is healthy.* Just one slice of carrot cake has 560 calories, that's the same as eating 14 pieces of bacon.

MYTH 487. | *Soy sauce is good for you.* Just one table spoon of soy sauce contains 38% of your daily recommended intake of salt.

MYTH 488. | *Cats always land on their feet.* Cats need time to readjust their body in free-fall, therefore, the shorter the fall, the less likely the cat will land on its feet.

MYTH 489. | *Daddy longlegs are the most poisonous spiders.* While they do look freaky, many spiders that belong to the daddy longlegs species, don't produce any venom at all. The types that do produce venom can cause a mild rash. Additionally, daddy longlegs are better classified as harvestmen rather than spiders.

MYTH 490. | *An undercover police officer has to tell you the truth if you ask them if they're a police officer.* Considering that their life usually depends on it, an undercover police officer does not need to tell you truthfully if he's a police officer or not.

MYTH 491. | *Don't eat fruit after a big meal because it'll rot as it waits for the meal to be digested.* The fiber found in fruit will actually aid in digestion.

MYTH 492. | *Tetanus comes from rust.* Tetanus comes from the bacteria Clostridium tetani, which lives in soil. Therefore, rusty nails are covered in this bacteria because they've, most likely, been outside for a very long time.

MYTH 493. | *Everyone in the Middle Ages smelled bad.* In the Middle Ages, everyone continued the Roman practice of communal bathing, and most towns in medieval Germany even had a communal bath where craftsmen would bathe together after work. Overall, people in the Middle Ages actually bathed often.

MYTH 494. | *Knights were chivalrous and brave warriors.* During the Middle Ages, knights were young but professional warriors who, when they weren't fighting in a war, were taking out their violent urges on the local population.

MYTH 495. | *Women were treated as cattle.* When the local population worked on farms, all of the household responsibilities were split between the husband and the wife. Therefore, by default, women and men were equals since the women had to the exactly the same things that the men had to do.

MYTH 496. | *Walt Disney's head was frozen.* While there were always wild rumors being thrown around about Walt Disney due to his eccentric nature, his death certificate states that he was cremated and the reason Disney didn't have a funeral for him is because he stated that he didn't want one before he died.

MYTH 497. | *Mozart was buried in a pauper's grave.* Mozart was actually quite well off during his life. His income of around 10,000 florins a year placed him at the top 5% of the population. While he did get himself into some debt during his life, he was actually buried in a common grave, that was custom for middle class people who didn't own their own plot of land, and not in a pauper's grave.

MYTH 498. | *Oscar Wilde died from syphilis.* There really is no evidence that Wilde ever had syphilis in his life. In fact, most historians actually argue that Wilde died from an ear infection.

MYTH 499. | *Edgar Allan Poe died from alcoholism.* Sources do state that Poe died after being found under bizarre circumstances, there really is no evidence that he was impaired. More likely sources state that his symptoms at the time line up with a rabies infection rather than anything else.

MYTH 500. | *Inbreeding between cousins creates a genetically mutated baby.* After recent studies, scientists now argue that inbreeding between cousins only increases the risk of birth defects by 2 to 3%, which is the same risk as a woman who has a child at the age of 41.

MYTH 501. | *The pull out method during sex is an unreliable birth control method.* Recent studies have found that the pull out method, if used perfectly, has a 96% success rate. When compared to the success rate of condoms, 98%, it doesn't seem too unreliable. On the other hand, when it's used improperly, the pull out method has a 82% chance of success, while condoms that fail have a 83% chance of success.

MYTH 502. | *A woman's first time having sex is extremely painful.* The truth is, if the girl and her partner approach the situation in a slow and relaxed manner, then there will be no pain.

MYTH 503. | *Tongue rolling is a genetic trait.* A study done in the 1950s showed that rolling your tongue isn't something that you're born with, but it's something that you can learn.

MYTH 504. | *Flat feet are a body defect and are prone to injury.* In Fort Benning in 1989, a study did a sample of 300 soldiers and found that the soldiers with flat feet were less prone to injury than those with normal arches.

MYTH 505. | *Turkeys drown in the rain.* The whole myth originated with turkeys being unintelligent enough that when it rained, they would stare up at the sky and the rain water would fill up their mouths, causing them to drown. In reality, during a rain storm, turkeys would do what every other animal does, and find shelter.

MYTH 506. | *There is an American flag on the Moon.* According to Buzz Aldrin, one of the astronauts who was on the Moon, he and Neil Armstrong accidentally placed the original American flag too close to their spacecraft, and when they took off, the flag was blown away.

MYTH 507. | *Stonehenge was built by druids.* Even though we're not really sure who did build Stonehenge, it definitely wasn't the druids. Carbon dating puts the finished monument centuries before the Celtic tribe with druid priests even arrived to Britain.

MYTH 508. | *An alcoholic is anyone that drinks a lot.* Alcoholism is a psychological dependence on alcohol to get your through life, rather than a byproduct of drinking a lot. People who drink to cope with problems and to manage stress are considered to be alcoholics.

MYTH 509. | *Certain wines should only be paired with certain food.* All that really matters is your personal preference. No one's taste buds will work in the same way, and as a result, no two people will have the same preference when it comes to which food they enjoy with which wine.

MYTH 510. | *Puking will sober you up and help you avoid a hangover.* Puking doesn't do anything to clear alcohol out of your system because most of it is already in there. Since alcohol works its way into your system so quickly, the only way to get rid of it by puking is to puke it out as soon as you drink it.

MYTH 511. | *Opening a window during a storm relieves pressure.* The pressure difference has been completely exaggerated, especially because a house doesn't work like an airplane. An airplane is air tight, which is why there has to be oxygen pumped into it at all times, while a house isn't. Houses have small holes and openings all around that allow air to come through.

MYTH 512. | *Overpasses protect you from tornados.* Taking cover under an overpass is more dangerous than just running away. Climbing up into the space under the corner of the bridge gets you higher up in the air, in exactly the perfect spot where the winds from the tornado accelerate. This means that you have placed yourself in the perfect spot for the tornado to pick you up and throw you around.

MYTH 513. | *Pets can predict earthquakes.* The only way that the pets may notice an earthquake before their owners is when they feel the ground shaking. Pets often have greater sensitivity to things happening around them so they will notice the ground shake a few seconds before a human does.

MYTH 514. | *Hunter-gatherers lived a hard life that was always near starvation.* Actually, it was the life of a farmer that was a lot more difficult than hunting for your food. The heavy manual labor needed to raise food at a farm was completely different for people who were used to a bohemian lifestyle who enjoyed hunting pray that was plentiful in number.

MYTH 515. | *The first Native Americans migrated from Siberia.* There isn't one single group that migrated over that distance to a new and uninhabited land. The fact is, migrations are done by many different groups of people from many different cultures and places. The first Native Americans are most likely a collection of many different groups migrating to a new land over time.

MYTH 516. | *You can hack any mainframe over the internet.* While a database with usernames and passwords can be accessed online, a mainframe will never be connected to any sort of public database. Companies and governments have their mainframes connected to a companywide intranet, and are very careful about them not being connected to public internet.

MYTH 517. | *LSD will make you insane.* In a study done in 1960, LSD was given to 2,000 people, half of who were known to be mentally ill or genetically predisposed to mental illness, and the other half being average people. After the test was done, only .13% of the subjects exhibited any sort of psychotic behavior, and all of which were already in the mentally ill category.

MYTH 518. | *Natural drugs aren't as bad for you.* Actually, natural drugs have a higher chance of killing you than artificially made drugs. With artificial drugs, you know what you're getting, however, with natural drugs, you never really know the potency of the drug and how hard it'll affect you. For example, opium, which is squirted out of a poppy, is highly addictive and can kill you easily if you take too much.

MYTH 519. | *PCP turns normal people violent.*
Research shows that PCP doesn't cause users to be
violent, unless they were already predisposed to
violent behavior.

MYTH 520. | *Gun suppressors can almost silence a
gunshot.* All a suppressor can actually do is make a
larger gun sound like a smaller gun. An unsilenced
gunshot is around 140 - 160 decibels, while a silenced
one is around 120 - 130 decibels, meaning that a gun
suppressor will not completely silence a gunshot.

MYTH 521. | *Coca-Cola will melt your stomach.*
While Coca-Cola does contain acid, so does a lot of
other food and drinks, such as orange juice, which is
also more acidic. The reason none of these foods have
already damaged your stomach is because the acids
are diluted enough to be safe for consumption.

MYTH 522. | *MSG burns your brain cells.* The only
way for MSG to affect you in any negative way
would be for you to eat a couple of hundred pounds
of it every single day.

MYTH 523. | *Cold water after a meal will give you
cancer.* Cold water after a meal will not give you
cancer, nor will warm water after a meal help you
prevent cancer or heart attacks.

MYTH 524. | *Margarine is actually plastic.*
Margarine isn't plastic, it's made from vegetable oil. It

was originally invented as a cheaper substitute for butter in 19th century France.

MYTH 525. | *Putting ice on a burn will make it go away.* Putting ice on a burn just inflicts more damage. A study done on rats with burns on their bodies, in which researchers compared different remedies, found that putting an ice cube on the burn for 10 minutes causes the most severe damage.

MYTH 526. | *Pirates wore eye patches to cover a missing eye.* Pirate wore eye patches to keep one eye adjusted to darkness while boarding another ship. This means that they only wore the patch before and during a raid.

MYTH 527. | *All pirate ships had a skull flag.* The black flag waving on a pirate ship meant that the pirates were willing to give quarter. When they were attacking, pirates would put up a completely red flag.

MYTH 528. | *Sailors became pirates because they wanted to be criminals.* The majority of pirates were originally sailors who left their jobs because of terrible work conditions. Only a very small number of pirates became pirates because they enjoyed the criminal lifestyle.

MYTH 529. | *Pirates buried their treasure.* Only three pirates buried their treasure before, and they never made maps for them. That's because they buried their treasure when they couldn't carry all of it with the intention of coming back in a few hours or days to collect it.

MYTH 530. | *Pirates mostly stole gold.* When pirates took over ships, they primarily stole salted fish and supplies that were going to the colonies. While gold and silver are nice, food was necessary to survive on the open sea.

MYTH 531. | *People in the Victorian area didn't have a lot of sex.* While people in the Victorian era didn't expose much of their skin in public, in private, they produced some of the most deviant forms of porn ever seen or heard of. Couples and even groups would act out in displays of incest, rape, pedophilia, BDSM, etc.

MYTH 532. | *Jewish people had sex through a sheet.* In fact, Jewish law prohibits clothed or covered sex.

MYTH 533. | *Asteroid belts are deadly.* While asteroid belts have millions of asteroids in them, the asteroids are miles apart from each other. NASA scientists even sent a probe through one and said that, due to the distance between asteroids, the odds of colliding with an asteroid were one in a billion.

MYTH 534. | *Meteorites are hot.* Meteorites travel through extremely cold temperatures of space for millions to billions of years. The only time that they're hot is when they enter the atmosphere at extreme speeds.

MYTH 535. | *Thomas Beatie is the world's first pregnant man.* The only reason why Beatie was pregnant was because he was born a woman and still had his female sex organs.

MYTH 536. | *Taking Aspirin prior to drinking will prevent hangovers.* A study by the American Medical Association found that ingesting aspirin slows the rate at which your body metabolizes alcohol. This increases blood alcohol levels, and makes the effects of alcohol last longer in the body.

MYTH 537. | *You can beat a breathalyzer test.* Absolutely nothing that you do will beat a breathalyzer test because nothing that you can do can get rid of the alcohol present on your breath.

MYTH 538. | *Christians were fed to lions and martyred in the Coliseum.* In fact, there are no authentic accounts of the Romans ever executing Christians in the Coliseum. However, that's not to say that Christians didn't suffer under the Romans as Emperor Nero persecuted them as arsonists, but that was before the Coliseum was even built.

MYTH 539. | *The Ancient Olympics were about physical ability and not endorsements and fame.* Every single aspect of modern games was present from the very beginning of the Olympiad. Ancient

Greek athletes were just as motivated by material gain and glory as today's athletes are.

MYTH 540. | *Spousal abuse is highest on Super Bowl Sunday.* There is no evidence that suggests that spousal abuse increases on Super Bowl Sunday, and some researchers argue that some men may be distracted by football, which makes them less likely to hit their wives.

MYTH 541. | *Washington, D.C., has skyscrapers.* The highest commercial building in Washington is only 12 stories tall. In fact, the tallest thing in Washington is the Washington Monument that is 329 feet tall.

MYTH 542. | *It's always winter in Moscow.* Just like many other cities in the world, Moscow has a winter season and a summer season. While their winters tend to last longer, it doesn't mean that they don't have scorching hot summers as well.

MYTH 543. | *It's always sunny in Australia.* Though much of Australia is dessert, there's plenty of snow to find during the winter seasons in the right parts. For example, it's not uncommon to see snow in Canberra, Australia during the winter months.

MYTH 544. | *Miami has a famous sign.* While the myth was created by popular movies such as Bad Boys and Transporter 2, the "Miami" sign was just created as a set prop for the movie and does not actually exist in real life.

MYTH 545. | *During World War II, Winston Churchill was the universally loved leader of the Allies.* Churchill seemed to have an almost insatiable urge to keep fighting in World War II, that extended even when the war was over. Since this meant that millions of men more would die, he became increasingly unpopular with the British military and British population.

MYTH 546. | *Franklin D. Roosevelt had knowledge about the Japanese attacking Pearl Harbor.* This was nothing more but a rumor that was used a smear campaign against FDR by his political opponents.

MYTH 547. | *Gun shots to the shoulder or leg are just flesh wounds.* A study done on 58 patients with gunshot wounds to the shoulder found that four months after the initial injury, 51 of them were suffering from a persistent pain due to vascular damage and about half of them ended up with complete loss of mobility in their arm.

MYTH 548. | *World War II was a technologically based war.* Even in World War II, the Soviet Army had at least 3.5 million horses in its services and deployed tens of thousands of mounted cavalrymen. Even the Germans had enough horses to outnumber vehicles by 3 to 1.

MYTH 549. | *The Nazis came very close to developing a Nuclear Bomb.* The Nazis weren't close to developing a Nuclear Bomb because the Reich was so disdainful of scientists who were capable enough to develop the Nuclear Bomb that they considered the whole field of study "Jewish physics," forcing the scientists out of Germany.

MYTH 550. | *If you let your anger out, you'll feel better.* Researchers say that letting your anger out doesn't work. In fact, it makes you more angry because the rush of anger that we let out becomes addicting, meaning that we are more likely to lash out as a mean of controlling our anger.

MYTH 551. | *Toilet waste is intentionally jettisoned from an aircraft.* All waste it collected in tanks and emptied on the ground by toilet waste vehicles. Blue ice that sometimes forms on a plane doesn't come from waste but by accidental leakage from the water tank.

MYTH 552. | *Car batteries stored on concrete discharge faster than on any other surface.* Early batteries might have done this due to being susceptible to moisture on the floor but modern batteries have impermeable polycarbonate cases that protect them from any moisture.

MYTH 553. | *Schizophrenia is the same as dissociative identity disorder, or having multiple personalities.* Schizophrenia is completely different than dissociative identity disorder because schizophrenia deals with people who hear and sometimes see things that are not there while dissociative identity disorder makes one person have multiple, different, personalities.

MYTH 554. | *Gyroscopic forces are required for a person to balance a bicycle.* Although gyroscopic forces can be contributing factors, studies have shown that the factors aren't required or even sufficient just by themselves.

MYTH 555. | *Air takes the same time to travel above and below an aircraft's wing.* This is a common fallacy in textbooks and non-technical reference books, however, the air moving over the top of an airfoil generating lift is always moving much faster than the equal transit theory would imply.

MYTH 556. | *The Ancient Greeks designed the Parthenon to deliberately match the golden ratio.* The Parthenon was complete in 438 B.C., which is more than a century before the first recorded mention of the golden ratio was made by Euclid.

MYTH 557. | *When an event with equally probably outcomes comes out the same way several times in succession, the other outcome is more likely next time.* This misconception is known as the gambler's fallacy and it often happens to people betting in a casino. For example, on a roulette wheel, if red comes up seven times in a row, the majority of people believe that black will come next. However, that's wrong, because statistical independence still holds, meaning that red has the same probability of coming out again as black does.

MYTH 558. | *James Watt invented the steam engine.* Watt only developed upon the first commercially successful Newcomen steam engine in the 1760s and 1770s, making improvements to its future usage.

MYTH 559. | *Guglielmo Marconi invented the radio.* Marconi didn't invent the radio, but he modernized it for public broadcasting and communication.

MYTH 560. | *There are dialysis machines that can be accessed in exchange for pull tabs on beverage cans.* While this rumor existed since the 1970s, the National Kidney Foundation has denied that any such machine exists, noting that 80% of the cost of dialysis in the United States is covered by Medicare.

MYTH 561. | *If you have eczema and you bathe, your skin will be dryer than before.* Studies have shown that bathing actually helps the skin for people with eczema.

MYTH 562. | *Having sex in the days leading up to a sporting event is detrimental to performance.* Actually, studies have shown that having sex prior to sporting events can elevate the levels of testosterone in males, which will help increase overall performance.

MYTH 563. | *The most dangerous sport in the world is American Football.* Actually, it's kite flying. In the last 10 years, kite flying has injured thousands of people and killed 460 in India. This is because kite runners coat their kites with steel and glass to help them fly, making the kites razor sharp and extremely dangerous.

MYTH 564. | *You can live a chemical-free life.* You can't live a chemical-free life because everything that we do, including breathing air, eating food and drinking water, is made out of chemicals. It doesn't matter if you live off the land or if you follow an organic diet, absolutely everything you do will be involved with some kind of chemical.

MYTH 565. | *Manmade chemicals are dangerous.* Whether a chemical is manmade or natural doesn't tell you anything about how dangerous the chemical might be. What is often the case with chemicals isn't the fact of if they're toxic or not, it's the quantity that you consume. For example, sodium thiopental, which is used for lethal injections, is found in almonds and apple seeds and is perfectly fine to consume at small amounts.

MYTH 566. | *Synthetic chemicals cause cancer.* This type of misconception is often found when researchers mention that an effect on cancer was seen in the presence of a chemical. This type of observation is just a correlation, and not necessarily a cause and effect link between the two.

MYTH 567. | *Chemical exposure can kill you.* We permanently live in constant exposure to various chemicals and have done so ever since life evolved on Earth, yet we are still alive to this day.

MYTH 568. | *Running shoes take weeks to break in.* Actually, if you buy good shoes, they should feel comfortable from the first moment you put them on.

MYTH 569. | *You should buy running shoes that tightly wrap your feet.* Feet expand on impact to help your body absorb shock. You should have about a thumb's width between the end of your longest toe and the end of your shoe, which is about a full size bigger.

MYTH 570. | *You'll stay the same shoe size your entire adult life.* Feet expand in both length and width as you get older so don't be surprised when you need to buy a bigger size of shoe.

MYTH 571. | *You would get drunk faster when an airplane is at cruising altitude.* Since planes are not pressurized to sea level, there's less oxygen in the air to begin with, which can make you feel drunk without you actually being drunk.

MYTH 572. | *You can get stuck on the toilet on a plane if you flush while sitting down.* You can get stuck if your body forms a perfect seal on the vacuum toilet. While it might sound simple, this is actually very difficult to do. However, even if you were to get stuck on the toilet, getting unstuck is as simple as getting up.

MYTH 573. | *Recirculated air in planes spreads disease.* Actually, the air circulates until it's drawn into the lower fuselage, where half of it is vented overboard. The other half is run through filters, then mixed with a fresh supply from the engines, and returned up to the cabin.

MYTH 574. | *Wearing seat belts can lower your chances of surviving a plane crash.* If you didn't wear your seatbelt, you would definitely be thrown out of your seat in a plane crash. This would cause much more damage to you and others around you then if you're strapped into the seat and have to unbuckle later on.

MYTH 575. | *Pilots can control airflow to keep passenger sedated.* Oxygen levels are determined by pressurization and pilots can't cut back on oxygen when they want to.

MYTH 576. | *Oxygen masks are decoys, meant to keep passengers calm before a crash.* Sometimes the cabin can lose pressure at 30,000 feet, where the air is not oxygen rich, meaning that the oxygen masks are a must for the safety of the passengers.

MYTH 577. | *Coffee stunts your growth.* In adults, researchers have found that increased caffeine consumption can limit calcium absorption, but the impact is so small that just a tablespoon of milk would offset the effects of an entire cup of coffee.

MYTH 578. | *Tequila makes people crazy.* Researchers found that alcohol will always be alcohol no matter which way it's made. Therefore, be it vodka or tequila, it will affect you in the exact same way.

MYTH 579. | *Bitcoins are worthless because they aren't backed by anything.* Bitcoin doesn't need anything to back its value up because, as the subjective theory of value states, anything can have value if it serves a purpose for someone.

MYTH 580. | *Bitcoin is illegal.* In March 2013, the United States Financial Crimes Enforcement Networked issued a new set of guidelines for virtual currency stating that, "a user of virtual currency is not a Money Service Businesses under Fin CEN's regulations and therefore is not subjects to MSB registration, reporting, and record keeping regulations."

MYTH 581. | *Bitcoin is untraceable.* Every single Bitcoin transaction that gets made is recorded at Blockchain.info.

MYTH 582. | *Bitcoin is safe and secure.* Actually, Bitcoins can be stolen and as the Mt. Gox scandal shows, as long as there's humans behind the scenes, corruption and greed will always be a factor.

MYTH 583. | *There can only ever be 21 million Bitcoins in existence and that isn't enough to go on.* Bitcoin can be divided by up to eight decimal places. So, while the value of one Bitcoin may rise high, we can deal with small portions such as 0.000000001 Bitcoins. After that, we can even deal with fractionally named Bitcoins, such as milibitcoins and nonbitcoins.

MYTH 584. | *Multigrain food is rich in whole grains.* Multigrain means that the food contains more than one type of grain, while whole grain means that the food contains all parts of the grain kernel, like the bran, germ and endosperm.

MYTH 585. | *Oranges have the most vitamin C.* Oranges actually have less vitamin C than many other common fruits and vegetables. For example, a cup of chopped red bell pepper has almost three times more vitamin C than an orange.

MYTH 586. | *The world's richest people inherited all their money.* Actually, 65% of the world's wealthiest individuals are self made, with 16% having only partially inheriting their wealth. Only 19% of the wealthiest people in the world have inherited their wealth and all 19% have the lowest net worth out of all the ultra high net worth individuals.

MYTH 587. | *The majority of rich people are investment bankers.* Only 19% of the richest people in the world are involved in the finance industry.

MYTH 588. | *You have to go to an Ivy League University to become part of the ultra wealthy.* Although Harvard has the most ultra wealthy as its alumni, the combined alumni from all Ivy League Universities only makes up about 3.5% of the worlds ultra wealthy population.

MYTH 589. | *The wealthy don't give to charity.* The average ultra wealthy philanthropist donates $25 million over his lifetime, with billionaires giving over $100 million.

MYTH 590. | *The world's ultra wealthy fly by private jet and own a huge yacht.* Only a very small portion of the ultra wealthy have a high enough net worth to afford the mega yachts and private planes.

MYTH 591. | *Checking your credit score too often will damage it.* Although it will hurt your credit score if many outside agencies get official copies of your credit report, checking your own credit score doesn't do anything to it.

MYTH 592. | *You don't need to get a flu vaccine if you got it the year before.* The main reason why yearly vaccination is needed is because the strains of the flu virus that are currently circulating change from the ones that were circulating last year.

MYTH 593. | *Getting the flu isn't a serious disease.* Actually, between 3,000 and 50,000 people in the United States die because of the flu every year. That's from more than 200,000 people that are admitted to hospitals every year.

MYTH 594. | *You can't turn off a smartphones tracking system.* Both the iOS and Android platforms allow the user to turn off location tracking through the settings. If they're still worried about being tracked, turn off data and it will shut down all location tracking applications.

MYTH 595. | *Big companies are monitoring your smartphone usage and scrutinizing your movements.* While big companies like Apple and Google do collect date from millions and millions of users, it would be extremely difficult and unprofitable to scrutinize a specific users movements from all the data that they receive.

MYTH 596. | *All wealthy people own homes.* While many wealthy people do own homes, many of them also rent. For example, many celebrities that travel often for work find it more financially sound to rent from their current location than to own homes in multiples places.

MYTH 597. | *All rich people are experts at money management.* The rich get richer by investing in a good financial advisor who will ensure that their money will be optimized for the future. Even billionaires like Mark Zuckerberg have a financial advisor, Divesh Makan, who helps him plan for the future.

MYTH 598. | *Rich people have never been bankrupt.* Many of the worlds wealthiest people have lost everything at some point. For example, Donald Trump has filed for corporate bankruptcy 4 times, yet is worth more today than he was before filing for bankruptcy the first time.

MYTH 599. | *The more you use your credit cards, the better.* Actually, FICO, the most popular type of credit score, favors a lower percentage of your credit utilization ratio. Meaning that, if your card has a $1,000 limit and you use $700 of it, that's a 70% CUR. For your credit score to be optimal, you would have to keep the CUR score around 10 - 25%, which would mean that you shouldn't use your credit card as much as you thought.

MYTH 600. | *Your demographics affect your credit.* Your education, income, gender, race, location or any other demographic data doesn't matter when it comes to your credit score.

MYTH 601. | *People grieve in five stages.* Mourning is different for everyone and, in fact, a Yale study shows that most people accept the death of a loved one immediately. The five stages of grieving put acceptance at the end but, it actually happens first, with more emotional pain followed within the weeks after the death.

MYTH 602. | *People with a high IQ are inherently smarter than everyone else.* IQ tests assess "symbolic logic", which includes things like problem solving, short term memory, and image manipulation. However, neuroscientists state that cognitive ability is much more complicated than solving self-contained problems. An IQ test simply measures how well you can write the test, not how well you can solve real life problems or your verbal intelligence, which are just some of the things that make up our cognitive ability.

MYTH 603. | *Women aren't as aggressive as men.* Researchers found that when you place a person in a situation where he or she doesn't have an individual identity, aggressive attitudes are amplified. When researchers ran a test that included playing an interactive video game that required killing others player by dropping bombs on them, they found that, under normal circumstances, men dropped far more bombs than women. However, when the groups were put into a situation where they didn't have an individual identity, the women dropped far more bombs than men.

MYTH 604. | *Women aren't as horny as men.* A recent study asked a group of women about their sexual behavior within a controlled environment. One group was told that their answers would be public and monitored and the other was told that their answers would be anonymous. The researchers found that when the women knew someone would see their answers, they reported their sexual behavior as half of that of the group who was told that their answers would be anonymous. What this means is that women feel pressured to adhere to societal views that they shouldn't feel as horny as men, but, when they are placed in anonymous environments, they will admit that their sexual urges come just as often as those of men.

MYTH 605. | *Only men like watching porn.* According to a recent study, women's brains react just as quickly to erotic images as men's do. In fact, their reaction is even stronger than a mans.

MYTH 606. | *Only women suffer from body image issues.* Men feel the exact same pressure to look as close to perfect as they can. A recent study done at Harvard university found that 25% of people with eating disorders are men.

MYTH 607. | *Women aren't as good as men in math.* Janet Hyde from the University of Wisconsin-Madison complied math test scores and SAT results from 7 million students, and found that there was no difference in scores between males and females.

MYTH 608. | *Most victims of domestic violence are women.* Women are more likely to abuse, stalk and attack their partner than men are. There have been hundreds of studies done with sample sizes of thousands of different people that have found that when couples resort to physical violence, it's often the woman who attacks the man first.

MYTH 609. | *Governments have to pay off their debts.* Governments don't have to pay off their debts because a government will never retire, and will have a stable and growing income. Because of this, there's no reason it ever needs to pay off its debt as it can pay off the interest on it for, essentially, forever.

MYTH 610. | *The government prints money whenever it wants.* The government can't print money whenever it wants. Instead, it has rules and guidelines which dictate when it will print money and under what conditions.

MYTH 611. | *Your sex life will get worse after marriage.* Recent studies show that married couples have a lot more sex than unmarried couples. In fact, married couples have higher sexual satisfaction, more diverse sex and sex more frequently.

MYTH 612. | *Men cheat more than women.* Studies show that women tend to cheat just as often as men. Cheating in and of itself has really nothing to do with gender and more about the individual who chooses to do it.

MYTH 613. | *The longer the penis, the better it will feel for the woman.* A UCLA study 3D printed a variety of different penises and found that women valued girth much more than length. The actual preferred length was 6.5 inches.

MYTH 614. | *The hymen is a barrier.* The hymen isn't a barrier, it's a small crescent shaped membrane at the base of the vaginal opening. It can be torn by a variety of non-sexual activities, but it's possible to have sex without it damaging as well. If torn, it can also heal itself.

MYTH 615. | *Wearing two condoms at once is more effective than wearing one.* Wearing two condoms at once is less effective because the layers rub against each other, which causes them to crack and break.

MYTH 616. | *The clitoris is the half inch nub of flesh at the top of a woman's vaginal opening.* Actually, that's just the external structure. The clitoral complex is a large internal structure that extends all the way around a woman's vagina and several inches back into her body. The entire structure is sensitive, and is theorized to be the source of the g-spot and vaginal orgasms.

MYTH 617. | *If a woman has sex too often, the tightness of her vagina with be altered.* The size, shape and tightness of a woman's vagina can't be altered in any way by frequent or vigorous sex, or by an abnormally large penis.

MYTH 618. | *Older people don't have sex.* Sex is a lifelong aspect of the human race and is not determined by age, physical appearance, health or functional ability. The large majority of people remain sexually active well into old age and regular sexual activity in the elderly is associated with good mental and physical health.

MYTH 619. | *Different sexual positions will influence your baby's gender.* It is impossible for any sexual positions to influence your baby's gender.

MYTH 620. | *All sexually transmitted diseases have symptoms.* Chlamydia, gonorrhea and herpes often don't show any type of symptoms yet it doesn't mean that you don't have them.

MYTH 621. | *You can change your penis size with pills.* You can't change your penis size with pills or exercises; the only way that you can change your penis size is with surgery.

MYTH 622. | *You won't get pregnant from sex as long as you do it in a hot tub or pool.* Although studies have shown that being in a hot tub for more than 30 minutes can lower your sperm count, there is nothing in the water that can kill off your sperm. Once even some sperm enters the vagina, it will try to find an egg and fertilize it.

MYTH 623. | *There are only two sexual orientations, straight or gay.* In 1948, Alfred Kinsey set up the "Kinsey Scale" which going from 0, or heterosexual, to 6, or homosexual, and theorized that sexuality was more of a gradation with people falling anywhere in between the two extremes. A recent study that surveyed 50,000 argued that over half of the world's population do not fit squarely in either the straight or gay category.

MYTH 624. | *Cutting wires is the last resort when defusing a bomb.* The last resort to defusing a bomb is often to send a robot in and shoot the bomb until it either falls apart or it explodes in a safe and covered area.

MYTH 625. | *You can get knocked out for a while and still stand up without a problem.* Doctors say that if you're ever knocked out for more than five minutes, you must go to the emergency room as there's a very good chance that you have severe brain injury.

MYTH 626. | *You wouldn't be badly hurt if you were thrown by an explosion.* While it's popular in movies for the hero to run away and then get thrown by a huge explosion behind him, real life is quite different. Anything that can create such a large explosion, would easily shred your body into pieces, even at a distance.

MYTH 627. | *If you land in a soft spot after a big fall you wouldn't suffer much damage.* Falls above 30 feet are almost always fatal, even if you land on something soft.

MYTH 628. | *Prides of lions have multiple females and only one male.* There are many instance of multiple males belonging to the same pride. Brothers, once they leave their natal pride, will often form a new pride together. Two or more brothers that are cast out into the savanna on their own, will look to take over a male's place in another existing pride.

MYTH 629. | *All male lions have manes.* In some parts of Africa, males have scanty manes or even no manes at all. One of the main theories behind this is that male lions lost their manes as a response to the extremely hot climate in the African savannah.

MYTH 630. | *Wild tigers are native to Africa.* Tigers are actually native to Asia, where they are presently found in 14 countries called the tiger range states.

MYTH 631. | *Tigers, like most cats, don't like water and are careful to avoid it.* Tigers like water and are excellent swimmers. Tigers also need to drink regularly, and they often slip into pools of water to cool off in the hot weather.

MYTH 632. | *Today's tigers are descendants of the prehistoric saber-toothed tigers.* Saber-toothed tiger species that we know from fossils are a completely difference species, not even remotely close to the modern tiger.

MYTH 633. | *Tigers will attack humans the second they get the chance.* Tigers actually go out of their way to avoid human contact.

MYTH 634. | *Tigers prefer small pray to large pray.* If given a choice, tigers will go for large pray because killing a larger pray is more energy efficient and will feed them for longer.

MYTH 635. | *White tigers are albino.* The actual color of the white tiger is due to a recessive gene and not because they are a true albino. Also, unlike albinos, white tigers have blue rather than pink eyes.

MYTH 636. | *All tigers are around the same size.* Depending on the subspecies and the habitat, tigers vary drastically in size and weight. For example, a Siberian male tiger may be four times heavier than a Sumatran female.

MYTH 637. | *Tiger hunts have a high success rate.* Actually, only 1 in 20 tiger hunts are successful.

MYTH 638. | *Tigers are good at climbing trees.* While lions are good at climbing trees, tigers are not, mainly due to being too heavy. For centuries, hunters in India used to put watch platforms in trees to ambush tigers.

MYTH 639. | *A male tigers territory is about the same as a female's.* The territory of a male tiger is seven times larger than that of a female. The primary cause of territoriality in males isn't to access food, it's to access females for breeding.

MYTH 640. | *Winter is mating season for tigers.* While winter may be preferred in certain habitats, tigers in India are conceived and born throughout the year.

MYTH 641. | *Every tiger can be identified by its pug marks.* The best that can be done with careful observation of pug marks is to identify a female from a male, in order to verify the presence of cubs. However, you can't identify each individual tiger by its pug marks.

MYTH 642. | *Tigers never move around during the day.* Depending on temperature conditions, the movements of the pray, it's possible to see tigers moving throughout the day.

MYTH 643. | *Tigers have slit pupils like house cats.* Tigers actually have round pupils because, unlike domestic cats who are nocturnal, tigers are crepuscular, as they hunt in the morning and evening.

MYTH 644. | *White tigers come from Siberia.* White tigers actually originate from India, specifically, Rewa in India.

MYTH 645. | *Black tigers don't exist.* Black tigers do exist as it's a simple case of melanism. Melanism also causes black jaguars and leopards, which are often called black panthers.

MYTH 646. | *Elephants love to eat peanuts.* Elephants spend anywhere from 16 to 18 hours a day eating. Peanuts are just too small to satisfy the elephants appetite.

MYTH 647. | *Elephants drink water through their trunks.* Elephants actually use their trunks to scoop up water before curling their trunks towards their mouths to drink it.

MYTH 648. | *Elephants are too heavy to swim.* Elephants love water and can smell it from five miles away. They are also good swimmers and have been known to use their trunks as snorkels.

MYTH 649. | *The abacus comes from China.* The device for performing operations was first used by the Egyptians around 2000 B.C. The word itself is derived from the Greek "abax", meaning a writing or ciphering tablet.

MYTH 650. | *In Great Britain, the monarch can simply decide to quit.* Actually, the king or queen must request permission to abdicate. Following the request, Parliament must draw up an article of abdication which states the full requirements and conditions for the royal resignation.

MYTH 651. | *Adam and Eve had two children.* The Bible states that they had three sons, Cain, Abel and Set, and that Adam fathered additional unspecified number of sons and daughters.

MYTH 652. | *Air has no weight.* Air has weight, for example, the total weight of the Earth's atmosphere is 5600 trillion tons.

MYTH 653. | *Air fresheners remove odor from the air.* Air fresheners work by covering the smell of the odor with an even stronger scent, which leaves the odor undetectable.

MYTH 654. | *Air pockets exist.* Air pockets don't exist and, since a plane needs air to fly, if a plane ever hit an actual air pocket, it would fall to the ground.

MYTH 655. | *The shadow of a flying plane is larger than the shadow of a grounded plane.* Both of the shadows are the same size as each of them would be as big as the plane itself.

MYTH 656. | *Landing produces the greatest tire wear for plane tires.* While it might seem extreme when the plane lands and the tires are seen smoking and screeching, the most wear that plane tires get are when the plane turns while on the ground.

MYTH 657. | *Brides walk down the aisle during a wedding.* Actually, the center section where brides walk during the wedding isn't called an aisle, it's called the nave.

MYTH 658. | *Alcohol is a stimulant.* Alcohol isn't a stimulant, it's a depressant. Due to this, its effect can vary from mental disorganization to death.

MYTH 659. | *Egyptians had a secret embalming technique that kept their mummies so well preserved.* The secret that the Egyptians had was Egypt itself and not any sort of technique. The fact that Egypt was hot and dry made it a perfect place to preserve their dead.

MYTH 660. | *The people vote for the President of the United States.* The President and Vice President are not elected by a direct vote of the people, they're actually chosen by the Electoral College. It's these electors, who receive the votes in a presidential election.

MYTH 661. | *The electric eel is an eel.* While it is shaped like an eel, an electric eel is actually a South American freshwater fish called the knifefish.

MYTH 662. | *The names England, Great Britain, British Isles, United Kingdom and the British Commonwealth are interchangeable.* Actually, the name aren't interchangeable as they refer to completely different political and geographic entities.

MYTH 663. | *Eye for an eye is meant to support revenge.* "Eye for an eye, tooth for a tooth," was actually intended as an attempt at equal and consistent justice amongst the noblemen and the peasants. It was meant to limit vengeful retaliation and not support it.

MYTH 664. | *The name "Great Danes" originated in Denmark.*

Great Danes were originally bred in Ancient Egypt as large dogs for royalty and they have nothing to do with Denmark. The Great Dane's name actually came from an old French word for the dog "grand Danois", but it's unknown why the French associated the dog with Denmark.

MYTH 665. | *Green apples make people sick.*

According to the United States Department of Agriculture, both green and red, or unripe and ripe, apples are digestible by the stomach as long as it is chewed sufficiently.

MYTH 666. | *There is only one species of horse.*

The Equus genus, the species to which the horse belongs to, has two subspecies. The first is equus ferus caballas, which is the domesticated horse we know off. The second is the Przewalski's horse, which is native to Mongolia.

MYTH 667. | *It's not good for a horse to let it graze on its own.*

Actually, the body of a horse has evolved specifically for grazing. When a horse grazes, the bottom jaw slides forward to ensure that the grass is properly grinded, which triggers the appropriate amount of salivation, aiding in the digestion process.

MYTH 668. | *The quality of a horse can be determined by its color.* The horses color and markings are purely genetic and don't have anything to do with the conformation or the temperament of the horse.

MYTH 669. | *White horses are albinos.* Horses actually have a "lethal white syndrome" that's often confused with albinism. Horses that are affected with the syndrome are born with blue eyes and entirely white coats.

MYTH 670. | *Horses are a lot like dogs.* Just because the two species are domesticated, doesn't mean that they are anything alike. For example, dogs are carnivorous while horses are herbivores. The same goes for how they are trained, dog training begins when the dog is just a puppy while a horse is trained for riding when it is at least 3 or even 5 years old.

MYTH 671. | *All horses sleep standing up.* While some horses do sleep while standing, many will sleep lying down. Horses have a physiological adaption that allows them to relax their body while lightly sleeping that won't lead them to collapsing. However, horses also need REM sleep like humans, and they can't achieve this while standing, so they will sleep lying down.

MYTH 672. | *A horse with a broken leg must be shot.* This was often the case before surgery came into play. However, with current medical technology, a horses leg can be mended, though at an expensive cost.

MYTH 673. | *The United States Highway system was designed to allow planes to land on them in emergencies.* This is a common urban legend that states that every five miles of highway must be straight to allow emergency airplane landings, but this is not the case.

MYTH 674. | *Johannes Gutenberg invented the printing press.* People in China and Korea were using movable type and the printing press centuries before Gutenberg. However, Gutenberg was the first European to use movable type, after bringing the technology over from China.

MYTH 675. | *Hitler created the Autobahn.* The Autobahn was built in 1931, two years before Hitler became Chancellor of Germany, and it was opened by the then Mayor of Cologne, Konrad Adanauer.

MYTH 676. | *Pong was the first video game.* While Pong was the first commercially successful video game, there was another game created in 1952, 20 years before Pong, called OXO. OXO was made by Alexander Douglas for his PhD thesis at Cambridge University, and it was nowhere near as commercially successful as Pong.

MYTH 677. | *You must warm your car up before driving.* Before, carburetors needed some time to warm up before you could drive. Now, all modern cars are ready to go as soon as you turn them on.

MYTH 678. | *Cars aren't as sturdy and safe as they used to be.* Modern cars are a lot sturdier and safer than older cars. Ever since the safety cells were invented in the 1970s by Bela Baranyi, who worked for Mercedes, modern cars have taken a much more safety conscious approach when being built.

MYTH 679. | *You must be able to see the flanks of your own car in your outside mirrors in order to have a reference.* Your outside mirrors are improperly adjusted if you can see the sides of your car. When they are correctly adjusted, they form a panoramic view.

MYTH 680. | *All season tires have more traction on wet roads.* Summer tires actually have more grip on a wet or dry surface than an all season tire. All season tires trade their wet and dry grip for mobility in snow or freezing temperatures.

MYTH 681. | *Engine oil must be changed every 3,000 miles.* Modern engine oil will effectively lubricate your engine for 10,000 miles or even more, depending on how you drive your car.

MYTH 682. | *Downshifting a manual car is done in order to slow down.* The entire purpose of downshifting in a manual car is to be in the proper gear to accelerate out of the next corner. Brakes do a much better job at slowing a vehicle down and are much cheaper to replace than transmissions.

MYTH 683. | *The purpose of antilock braking systems (ABS) is to shorten stopping distance.* The entire purpose of ABS was to give the driver the ability to steer around danger and not spin out completely as they stomped on their brakes.

MYTH 684. | *A tire can explode if you exceed the "max pressure" number on the sidewall.* The max pressure number refers to the cars load carrying capability, not its burst pressure. The burst pressure of the tire is far beyond the max pressure number.

MYTH 685. | *When you're renting a car, you need to buy additional coverage for the rental car.* In the United States, the insurance policy that you have for your car also covers the rental.

MYTH 686. | *It's illegal to jailbreak an iPhone.* The Library of Congress states that jailbreaking doesn't constitute breaking copyright law and you are free to jailbreak any product that you have purchased.

MYTH 687. | *The iPhone dominates the mobile platform.* While this is true if you count all the Apple devices ever sold, but if you account for the ones that are currently in use, Android is ahead of Apple.

MYTH 688. | *The iPhone screen scratches easily.*
The current iPhone screen is made out of Gorilla
Glass, which is a chemically strengthened piece of
glass that's 20 times stiffer and 30 times harder than
plastic.

MYTH 689. | *Tape your windows before a
hurricane.* Taping your windows won't do anything to
help keep it in place when a serious hurricane blows
through. In fact, the duct tape may even create larger
shards of glass that can seriously injure you.

MYTH 690. | *Everything that moves, will eventually
come to a stop.* This statement is wrong because
Newton's First Law of Motion states that, "everything
at rest will stay at rest, and everything in motion will
stay in motion, unless acted upon by an external
force."

MYTH 691. | *A continuous force is needed for
continuous motion.* Actually, the force that you apply
to keep an object moving is only to counteract the
frictional force that the object is going against.

MYTH 692. | *An object is hard to push because it's
heavy.* The reason a heavy object is hard to push isn't
because of its weight, it's because of its inertia, which
is the objects resistance to change in motion.

MYTH 693. | *Heavier objects fall faster than lighter
ones.* All objects moving through air experience air
resistance. This resistance is proportional to the area

of the objects in the direction of motion. For lighter objects, the weight is comparable to the air resistance, which means that it will have a big effect on how fast the object lands.

MYTH 694. | *Evolution is a theory about the origin of life.* Evolution is a theory that primarily looks at how life has changed after its origin, not where it originated from. While the origin is still widely speculated, evolution looks at how life branches off from its point of origin.

MYTH 695. | *Organism are always getting better and better.* All creatures evolve to adapt to their environment, but some creatures have their environment changed so rapidly that they can't adapt fast enough, meaning that their evolution wasn't better suited to their current environment.

MYTH 696. | *Evolution means that life changed by chance.* Natural selection is far from random. For example, many water based animal need speed to survive and reproduce, therefore, they developed the ability to move faster under water which helped them be more suited to their environment, and be more likely to survive. This didn't happen by chance, it happened because the organism needed to survive.

MYTH 697. | *Natural selection means that organisms are trying to adapt.* Organisms don't try to adapt, they change through genetics that get passed to their offspring.

MYTH 698. | *Evolution is just a theory.* While most people understand the word "theory" as a "guess" that scientists made; in the scientific community, a theory is a well substantiated idea that explains certain aspects of the natural world.

MYTH 699. | *Gaps in the fossil records disprove evolution.* Actually, there are some organisms who don't fossilize well enough or exist in conditions that are good enough to allow the process of fossilization to take effect. This doesn't mean that just because the organism wasn't fossilized that evolution still doesn't have plenty to back it up.

MYTH 700. | *All of Africa is made up of rural regions.* Africa is made up of rural and urban regions. Africa has many forms of modern architecture and infrastructure, such as sky scrapers and sprawling cities.

MYTH 701. | *Most of Africa is a desert.* Africa is home to the Sahara desert but it only covers the third of the continent. The rest of the region is made up of fertile lands and bodies of water.

MYTH 702. | *Africa is a wide stretch of rain forest.* Only parts of the guinea cost and Zaire River basin are covered with rain forests. The rest of the forested areas have been cleared for towns, cities and farming communities.

MYTH 703. | *Africa has one homogenous culture.*
Every single country in Africa has a different culture
within it. While Africa does have many ethnic groups
that live amongst each other in modern times, each of
these groups comes from a different and completely
unique set of cultural beliefs.

MYTH 704. | *Wild animals roam the streets in
Africa.* Wild animals live in very controlled regions.
Africa is home to many different species of wild
animals and birds that are largely controlled in
wildlife reserves. It would be extremely rare to see
any wild animal roaming a modern city in Africa.

MYTH 705. | *Research on animals is not relevant to
people because animals are different from people.* All
mammals descended from common ancestors,
therefore, humans are biologically very similar to
other mammals. For example, vitamins work in the
same way in animals as they do in people, so research
on guinea pigs has led us to the discovery of how
vitamin C works.

MYTH 706. | *Animal research is not relevant
because people and animals suffer from different
illnesses.* Many veterinary medicines are the same as
those used for human patients. For example, animals
can naturally get illnesses such as cancer, heart
failure, asthma, rabies and malaria and all of them are
treated in the same way and with the same medicine
as human patients.

MYTH 707. | *Animal testing doesn't work and causes side effects in drugs.* Medicine is only tested on animals after extensive screening is done by computers. After the computer tests clear, animal tests show exactly how the medicine reacts in the living body and the effects that it has. After the medicine passes the testing on a living body, it's tested on volunteer human patients, so animal testing definitely does work as it's a part of a chain of events that need to take place for creation of a new medicine. Also, it doesn't cause side effects in drugs because animal testing is the time when any side effects are found.

MYTH 708. | *Medicines that work for people are toxic to animals.* This myth began when it was found that penicillin was toxic to guinea pigs. However, what wasn't stated is that it was only toxic at very high doses, which is the same effect that long term penicillin use does to human patients.

MYTH 709. | *Side effects of medicine are the major cause of hospital deaths.* A large number of deaths related to medicine is not caused by side effects, but by abnormal doses, both accidental and deliberate, being given to the patients. Even still, death caused by medicine is not the major cause of hospital deaths.

MYTH 710. | *Animal research hasn't made any contribution to medical progress.* Actually, insulin was discovered in dogs in the 1920s by Banting and Best which contributed a lot to medical progress. Before insulin was discovered, there really was no treatment for people with diabetes or for animals with diabetes.

MYTH 711. | *25 years of primate research has failed to find any sort of treatment for AIDS.* Primate research was crucial in identifying the virus, developing diagnostic tests, and producing therapies such as antiretrovirals that have helped many people who are living with AIDS, live a longer life.

MYTH 712. | *Animal research is a cheap and easy option for research.* Animal research and testing is very, very expensive due to needing a very large staff to look after the animals welfare. There are veterinarians on call all the time and all animal technicians must spends months in training so that they are ready to look after the animal that the medicine is being tested on.

MYTH 713. | *There are no laws or regulations that protect animals used for research purposes.* Many Westernized countries have national legislation that protects and looks after the welfare of animals that are used for research. The United Kingdom is well known for having some of the most comprehensive regulations that cover the welfare of animals used for research.

MYTH 714. | *Animals used for research suffer a lot of pain.* By law, researchers have to minimize the suffering of animals that they use for research. This is done by using anesthetic to alleviate pain during a procedure. Also, it's in the researchers best interest to make sure that the animal doesn't suffer as stressed animals are less likely to produce reliable results.

MYTH 715. | *Benjamin Franklin discovered electricity when his kite was struck by lightning in 1752.* Electricity was already well known at that time, Franklin was just trying to prove the electrical nature of lightning.

MYTH 716. | *Cinderella wore glass slippers.* More than 500 versions of the fairy tale exists, dating back to the 9th century, and in each version, Cinderella has a magic ring or magic slippers made out of gold, silver or some other rare metal, but they are never made out of glass.

MYTH 717. | *Lady Godiva rode naked through the streets of Coventry, England.* There are no legitimate historical accounts that Lady Godiva, the wife of Leofric, Earl of Mercia, ever rode naked through the streets of Coventry, England. In fact, the first references appears nearly 200 years after her death.

MYTH 718. | *You don't need to exercise your cat.* You do need to exercise your cat because cats need physical activity to keep healthy. Keeping your cat indoors all the time will make it gain weight and, ultimately, be miserable.

MYTH 719. | *Cats are immune to rabies.* Cats can carry rabies and should be vaccinated regularly.

MYTH 720. | *Introverted people don't like to talk.*
Introverted people like to talk, but just when they
have something to say. They don't like small talk but
if they're talking about something that they're
interested in, they can talk for as long as an
extroverted person.

MYTH 721. | *Introverted people are shy.* Shyness
is completely different than being an introvert.
Introverts aren't afraid of people, they just need a
reason to interact.

MYTH 722. | *Introverted people are arrogant.*
While introverts come across as cold, it's not because
they're arrogant, but because they're often
preoccupied with thinking and processing information
internally.

MYTH 723. | *You can get HIV by being around
people who are HIV positive.* You can't catch HIV by:
breathing the same air as someone who is HIV
positive, touching a toilet seat or doorknob handle
after an HIV positive person, drinking from the same
water fountain, hugging, kissing, or shaking hands
with someone who is HIV positive, sharing eating
utensils with the person or using gym equipment with
an HIV positive person.

MYTH 724. | *New drugs let HIV positive people
live completely normal lives.* Many of the new HIV
drugs are very expensive and have serious side effects

for the people who take them. Also, none of the drugs is an actual cure.

MYTH 725. | *You can get HIV from mosquitoes.* Several studies have shown that there is no evidence that you can get HIV from mosquitoes. When insects bite, they don't inject the blood of the person or animal that they have last bitten and even if they did, HIV lives for only a short time inside an insect.

MYTH 726. | *If you're receiving treatment, you can't spread HIV.* HIV treatments can reduce the amount of the virus in your blood but the virus can still hide in other areas of the body. It's absolutely essential that you use condoms when having sex because there's a still a good chance that you can pass the virus to another person.

MYTH 727. | *You can't get HIV from oral sex.* While oral sex is less risky than other forms of sex, the HIV virus can still pass from one person to the other.

MYTH 728. | *You can tell if another person has HIV.* HIV doesn't show symptoms for many years and the only way to know if another person has HIV is for the person to get tested.

MYTH 729. | *The Obama administration gives people on welfare free cell phones through the Lifeline program.* The Lifeline program started in 1984 under the Reagan administration. Discounts on prepaid wireless plans were added in 2005 by the Bush administration and, in 2008, eligible households were also able to choose between receiving discounts on one landline or wireless phone service. Eligible households can also receive a cell phone, but that's provided by the service provider and not the government.

MYTH 730. | *The Lifeline program is funded by taxpayers.* No federal money goes towards the funding of the Lifeline program. The entire program is funded by telecommunications companies by having their customers pay a Universal Service fee on their monthly bill.

MYTH 731. | *Science is just a collection of facts.* Actually, science is a body of knowledge and a process that helps us discover how the world works.

MYTH 732. | *There is one single "scientific method" that all scientists use.* The Scientific Method is often taught in science based courses as a very simple way of understanding the basics of scientific testing. However, it's a grossly oversimplified representation of how scientists and researchers use science to build knowledge.

MYTH 733. | *The process of science doesn't involve creativity.* Scientists argue that creative thinking is the most important skill to have as a scientist and a researcher. A scientist must have creative thinking to come up with an alternative hypothesis or to make a new way of testing an old idea.

MYTH 734. | *Scientific ideas are absolute and never change.* Even established scientific ideas are sometimes modified based on new evidence and new perspective that are introduced. Some scientific ideas tend to change quickly as scientists and researchers test different explanations when they try to figure out which is the most accurate.

MYTH 735. | *Because scientific ideas change so quickly, they can't be trusted.* Ideas that are at the cutting edge of research change quickly because scientists test out many different possible explanations. This is a normal part of science, and all scientific ideas are supported by a lot of evidence and are very reliable as a reference.

MYTH 736. | *Only brown chickens lay brown eggs.* The shell of any egg starts off white and the pigment is added as the egg travels through the chicken. The color of the shell at the end depends entirely on the breed of chicken that it comes from.

MYTH 737. | *You can tell what color eggs a hen will lay by her earlobes.* You can't tell what color egg the chicken will lay by looking at her earlobes. The only way you can even guess what color the egg will be is by looking at the breed of the chicken.

MYTH 738. | *Hens will only lay an egg if there's a rooster around.* A chicken produces an egg whether or not there's a rooster in the flock as it's part of her natural cycle. However, the egg will never be fertile unless there's a rooster around to fertilize it.

MYTH 739. | *Fertile eggs are not safe to eat.* It's safe to eat an egg which has been fertilized as the fertilized egg just has the cell which could turn into a chick, under right circumstances, and everything else about it is the same as an unfertilized egg.

MYTH 740. | *Sharks are not important for the ocean's ecosystem.* Sharks help maintain the balance of life as they keep the marine animal populations in check. Sharks mainly feed on the sick and weak, which helps the prey population stay healthy.

MYTH 741. | *All sharks eat humans.* Humans are not a sharks primary food source and every time a shark is involved with a human, it's because it's already hunting for a similar sized pray as a human, such as a dolphin or seal.

MYTH 742. | *All sharks are large with a mouth full of razor sharp teeth.* There are more than 400 different species of sharks and they come in a large variety of shapes and sizes. Some are 8 inch long deepwater dogfish and others are massive 40 foot long whale sharks. Not all sharks have a mouth full of sharp teeth either; for example, the basking shark has tiny teeth that it doesn't even use for feeding.

MYTH 743. | *Down syndrome is a rare disorder.* Down syndrome is the most common genetic condition. 1 in every 691 babies in the United States is born with Down Syndrome and there are more than 400,000 people living with the condition in the United States.

MYTH 744. | *People with Down Syndrome have a very short life span.* Life expectancy for people with Down Syndrome has increased by a lot in recent years, with the average life expectancy approaching people without the condition.

MYTH 745. | *Down Syndrome runs in the family.* Down syndrome is hereditary in only 1% of the cases. For the other 99% of the cases, it's completely random and is only known as a factor in mothers who have children over the age of 35.

MYTH 746. | *Children with Down Syndrome must be placed in segregated special education programs.* Actually, children with Down Syndrome have been included in regular academic classrooms across the United States. People living with Down Syndrome have graduated from high school with regular diplomas and participated in various postsecondary academic institutions.

MYTH 747. | *Down Syndrome can never be cured.* Research on Down Syndrome has identified the gene on chromosome 2 that cause the characteristics of Down Syndrome. Scientists and researchers feel that they could improve, correct or prevent all of the problems associated with Down Syndrome in the future if they identified the condition early enough.

MYTH 748. | *Native Americans were savages that hungered for war.* Many Native American tribes were peaceful and only went to war after Europeans came to America and upset the balance between the tribes. The Europeans then launched a massive propaganda campaign to paint the Natives as savages that had to be killed and couldn't live amongst the European population.

MYTH 749. | *Natives weren't as advanced as Europeans.* Native Americans had a very advanced society with medicine, trading, farming and many other common advancements that the Europeans had. However, their culture was very different than the Europeans, which led to the Europeans labeling them as primitive.

MYTH 750. | *Native Americans abused drugs.* Native Americans did smoke a drug called peyote, but it wasn't for recreational purposes. The drug was mainly used in religious and ritual instances.

MYTH 751. | *All Native Americans lived in teepees.* There were many different forms of dwellings that were used by different tribes in America. Teepees were used by natives who travelled regularly, because they're easy to break down, but many tribes had much larger and more permanent dwellings as well.

MYTH 752. | *Native American medicine was primitive.* When Europeans first came to America, their medicine wasn't much more advanced than that of the Natives, it was just different. Much of the herbal remedies that the natives used have actually been found to be effective, and some of the modern medicine that we have today comes from further research into the plants that the Natives had used for generations.

MYTH 753. | *Native Americans also have royalty.* Chiefs were not placed in power from birth, they were chosen for their leadership skills almost entirely. While their families were treated well, they were not the same as royalty as Native American culture does not create social divides like that.

MYTH 754. | *Native Americans worshipped nature.* Natives have a tremendous amount of respect for the Earth and the nature found on it. They don't specifically worship the nature itself but their religious beliefs are very in tune with it.

MYTH 755. | *All Native Americans still live on reserves.* As of 2008, 40% of Native Americans live on reserves while 60% has assimilated into American society. The conditions of the reserves are extremely bad, which explains why many choose to leave.

MYTH 756. | *If you agree to donate your organs, the hospital staff won't work as hard to save your life.* When you're at the hospital for treatment, the doctors and hospital staff will focus entirely on saving your life. Just because you have agreed to donate your organs doesn't mean that the hospital staff will suddenly let you die just to harvest your organs.

MYTH 757. | *Women are most likely to be raped outside by strangers in dark alleyways.* Actually, only 10% of rapes are committed by strangers with 90% of rapes being committed by men who are known to the woman.

MYTH 758. | *Rape only happens to young and attractive women.* Women of all ages, classes, cultures, abilities, sexuality, race and faith are raped. When a person rapes, it is an act of violence and not sex.

MYTH 759. | *Men of certain races and backgrounds are more likely to rape.* There is no typical image of a rapist. Studies show that men who commit rape come from different economic, ethnic, racial and social groups.

MYTH 760. | *Once a man is sexually aroused, he can't help himself so he rapes a woman.* Almost all rapes are planned well in advance. Rapes are also committed by more than one person at a time. Men can control their urges and they rape not for sexual gratification but to dominate, violate and control the woman.

MYTH 761. | *Men who rape don't have the opportunity to have sex with willing partners.* More than 1 in 5 women are raped by their partners or their husbands. This means that men who rape are just as likely as any other man to be in a relationship with a woman.

MYTH 762. | *Some people can't be hypnotized.* Everyone has the ability to be hypnotized because it's a natural, normal state that each of us enter at least twice every single day, once when we wake up and once when we fall asleep.

MYTH 763. | *You can be hypnotized to do things against your will.* The person who is hypnotizing you can't make you do anything against your will. During a hypnotic session, a person is completely aware of everything that is going on, all the person who is hypnotizing you can do is guide you, but you can still reject any of his or her suggestions.

MYTH 764. | *When you're hypnotized, you always tell the truth.* You can lie when you're hypnotized just as easily as when you're awake. Hypnosis just gives you a deeper access to your unconscious, so you might be able to tell even more creative lies when you're hypnotized as opposed to when you're awake.

MYTH 765. | *You won't remember anything the hypnotist said.* Being hypnotized doesn't mean that you will enter some unconscious like trance and not remember anything that's happened to you while you were in it. While everyone experiences hypnosis differently, everyone is consciously aware of what was said to them and what happened around them.

MYTH 766. | *A person can get stuck in a hypnotic trance forever.* No one has ever been stuck in a hypnotic trance because hypnosis is a naturally occurring state that we enter and exit during any normal day.

MYTH 767. | *Intelligent people can't be hypnotized.* Studies suggest that people who have above average intelligence are more capable of concentration and have a greater capacity of creativity, which usually means that they will have a much easier time entering a hypnotic trance.

MYTH 768. | *A person who is hypnotized is asleep or unconscious.* The state of hypnosis might seem like sleep from the physical point of view but from the mental standpoint, the person is relaxed and may even be fully alert. They are in a comfortable state where they can talk, think and even move if they have to.

MYTH 769. | *If you have cancer, eating sugar will make it worse.* While research has shown that cancer cells consume more sugar than normal cells, no studies have shown that eating sugar will make your cancer worse. However, eating a sugar rich diet may contribute to weight gain, which is associate with developing seven different types of cancer.

MYTH 770. | *Artificial sweeteners cause cancer.* There have been numerous studies done on the safety of all the different types of artificial sweeteners and researchers haven't found any evidence to suggest that they cause cancer in people.

MYTH 771. | *Cancer is contagious.* The only situation in which cancer can spread from one person to another is in the case of organ or tissue transplants. However, in any normal case, cancer is not a contagious disease that can spread from person to person.

MYTH 772. | *Cancer surgery can cause cancer to spread in the body.* The chance that surgery will cause cancer to spread to other parts of the body is extremely low. Surgeons use special methods and take steps to prevent cancer cells from spreading during surgeries.

MYTH 773. | *Cancer can get worse if it's exposed to air.* Exposure to air won't make tumors grow faster or cause cancer to spread to other parts of the body.

MYTH 774. | *Cell phones cause cancer.* Cancer is caused by genetic mutations, and the low frequency energy that cell phones emit, does not damage genes.

MYTH 775. | *Power lines cause cancer.* Power lines emit both electric and magnetic energy. However, the electric energy emitted by power lines is easily countered and weakened by walls and other physical objects. The magnetic energy is a low frequency form of radiation that's not powerful enough to damage genes and cause cancer.

MYTH 776. | *Herbal products can cure cancer.*
Some studies suggest that alternative therapies,
including herbs, can help patients cope with the side
effects of cancer treatment, but herbal products aren't
effective at treating cancer. In fact, some herbal
products can even be harmful when taken during
chemotherapy because they interfere with the way the
treatments work.

MYTH 777. | *If someone in your family has cancer,
you'll likely get it too.* Only 5-10% of cancers are
inherited from a person's parents. The majority of
cancers are caused by harmful changes or mutation to
a person's genes. These mutations are a natural result
of aging and exposure to various environmental
factors.

MYTH 778. | *Deodorants cause breast cancer.*
Studies done on this very topic have found no
evidence that links the chemicals typically found in
deodorants with changes in breast tissue.

MYTH 779. | *Using hair dye increases the risk of
cancer.* There is no scientific evidence that hair dye
increases the risk of cancer. However, some studies
suggest that hairdressers and barbers who are
regularly exposed to large quantities of hair dye and
other chemicals may have an increased risk of bladder
cancer.

MYTH 780. | *Getting too many vaccines could overwhelm a child's immune system.* Children are exposed to 700 foreign substances that trigger an immune response every single day. Their bodies constantly face things that attack their immune systems. In fact, scientific evidence even shows that giving several vaccines at the same time has no adverse effect on a child's immune system.

MYTH 781. | *You can swallow your tongue during a seizure.* It's physically impossible for anyone to swallow their tongue.

MYTH 782. | *You should force something into the mouth of someone who is having a seizure.* If you force anything into the mouth of someone who's having a seizure then you run the risk of chipping their teeth, puncturing their gums or even breaking their jaw. What you do is gently roll the person to the side and put something soft under their head to protect them from getting injured.

MYTH 783. | *You should restrain someone who's having a seizure.* Never try to restrain someone who is having a seizure. The seizure will run its course no matter what and you can't do anything about it.

MYTH 784. | *Epilepsy is contagious.* You can't catch epilepsy like a disease from another person.

MYTH 785. | *Achilles' biggest vulnerability was always his heel.* Actually, Homer originally described

Achilles' weak spot as his pride. However, the story was changed as it was retold over the next 600 years into the story we know today, that his mother held him by the ankle and dipped him in the Styx River to make him immortal.

MYTH 786. | *Every soldier prayed to Ares to help him in battle.* Ares was actually considered dangerous to have on your side. The Greeks believed him wildly unpredictable and looked at him as a liability in the Trojan War.

MYTH 787. | *ADHD only occurs in children.* Most people don't outgrow ADHD and continue to struggle with the disorder well into their adulthood.

MYTH 788. | *All microbes are bad.* The vast majority of microbes are harmless to human health. Others, are actually beneficial, such as the microbes that metabolize toxic chemicals and others that we use for cleaning and attacking pathogens.

MYTH 789. | *All E.coli bacteria is dangerous.* In fact, there are strains of E.coli that help with normal human digestive processes. Most people carry this type of strain in their guts all the time without getting sick.

MYTH 790. | *The appearance of autism is relatively new.* Autism was first described by Leo Kranner in 1943, but the earliest case of a child known to have had autism was written in 1799.

MYTH 791. | *Autism is a mental health disorder.*
Autism is a neurological disorder. Studies done on
people with autism have found that abnormalities
exist in brain structure and neurotransmitter levels.

MYTH 792. | *Autism is caused by poor parenting.*
In the 1950s, it was assumed that autism was caused
by emotionally distant parents. However, studies
since then have debunked that myth, but we are still
unsure of what exactly causes it.

MYTH 793. | *People with autism are violent.*
Violent acts from autistic people come from sensory
overload or emotional distress. Otherwise, it's very
unusual for autistic individuals to act out violently or
to pose any danger to society.

MYTH 794. | *All autistic people have savant
abilities.* Only about 10% of autistic people have
savant abilities. Many others have splinter skills,
which are skills in one or two areas that are above
their overall performance abilities.

MYTH 795. | *Autistic people lack empathy.* Autistic
people feel as much, if not more, empathy than
average people. However, they find it much harder to
express it in a way that others would recognize it.

MYTH 796. | *Autism can be cured.* There is no
known cure for autism.

MYTH 797. | *Scientists disagree about whether humans are causing the Earth's climate to change.* There is a scientific consensus that human activities are changing the Earth's climate. In fact, scientists overwhelmingly agree that the Earth is getting warmer and that this trend is directly caused by people.

MYTH 798. | *A gay couple will raise gay children.* There is no evidence that having gay parents will make the child gay. In fact, children that are raised by gay parents have the same chance of being gay as if they were raised by heterosexual parents.

MYTH 799. | *It's good to have a sports drink after you exercise.* Plain water is the best and most sufficient liquid to quench your thirst and replenish any fluids you have lost.

MYTH 800. | *Bees gather honey from flowers.* Honey bees collect nectar from flowers, they then convert that nectar into honey. Therefore, they don't directly gather honey from flowers but they do collect the key ingredient needed for honey.

MYTH 801. | *Insects have six legs attached to their abdomen.* In a majority of insects, their legs are attached at the thorax and not the abdomen.

MYTH 802. | *You can tell the age of a lady bug by counting the number of spots on its wings.* While lady bugs species can be told apart by the markings on their wings, the spots on the wings won't tell you anything about their age.

MYTH 803. | *Insects live on land.* There are many insects that live near and even in the water. For example, caddisflies, stoneflies, mayflies, dragonflies and damselflies all spend a part of their lives living in fresh water bodies.

MYTH 804. | *Spiders, insects and ticks are all bugs.* In a entomological sense, a bug is a member of the order Hemiptera. Cicadas, aphids, hoppers and stink bugs are all bugs, but spiders, ticks, beetles and flies aren't.

MYTH 805. | *It's illegal to harm a praying mantis.* The praying mantis isn't endangered nor is it protected by law. However, people consider the prayer-like stance of the praying mantis a sign of good luck, and thought that harming a mantis would be a bad omen.

MYTH 806. | *Insects try to attack people.* Insects don't intent to inflict pain on people. Bees sting defensively when they feel threatened and some insects, like mosquitoes, are just looking for a meal.

MYTH 807. | *All spiders make webs.* While many spiders do spin webs of silk, hunting spiders such as wolf spiders and jumping spiders, pursue their prey rather than entrap them in a web.

MYTH 808. | *Insects aren't really animals.* Insects are arthropods that belong to the animal kingdom just like we do.

MYTH 809. | *A daddy longlegs is a spider.* A daddy longlegs, or harvestmen, lack seven characteristics that every spider has. The two most important characteristics are the fact that spiders have two distinct body parts, the cephalothoraxes and abdomen, while a daddy longlegs has one and spiders posses silk and venom glands while a daddy longlegs doesn't.

MYTH 810. | *If it has eight legs, it's a spider.* Actually, many insects that are part of the Arachnida class are characterized by having eight legs in total.

MYTH 811. | *If you find a bug in the sink or tub then it came up from the drain.* Insects are drawn to the more humid environment of a bathroom or kitchen. Once an insect comes down the slop of a sink or bathtub, it has a hard time crawling back up and ends up stranded near the drain.

MYTH 812. | *Insects sing with their mouths.* What we refer to songs are actually mating and defensive calls of an insect. Insects can't produce the same sounds that we can because they don't have vocal cords. Instead, they produce sounds by using different parts of their body to make vibrations. For example, crickets rub their forewings together.

MYTH 813. | *Small insects with wings will mature into adults.* If an insect already has wings then it's an adult, no matter how small the insect may be.

MYTH 814. | *Plasma TVs need to have their plasma changed every couple of years.* You don't need to change the ionized gases inside plasma displays after buying your plasma TV. Even if you did have to, the top tier plasma brands that are currently on the market have a half life of 100,000 hours, which is more than enough to outlast your life.

MYTH 815. | *Psychopaths are insane.* The American Psychiatric Association considers psychopathy to be a personality disorder and it argues that psychopaths know the difference between right and wrong and, therefore, are not insane.

MYTH 816. | *All mass murderers are psychopaths.* The large majority of adults who kill multiple people aren't psychopaths but depressive homicidal individuals who suffer from serious mental illnesses.

MYTH 817. | *All psychopaths are violent.* While the collection of traits and behaviors that characterize psychopaths makes people think that they are violent, there is plenty of room for nonviolent behavior and there are plenty of psychopaths who are not violent, but simply lack empathy.

MYTH 818. | *Prisons are full of psychopaths.* Prisons aren't full of psychopaths but they are full of people who suffer with antisocial personality disorder. 75% or more of prisoners in the United States are diagnosed with this disorder.

MYTH 819. | *Depression isn't a real illness.*

Depression is a complex disorder that has psychological, social and biological origins. Depression is a mental illness that must be treated in various ways and it shouldn't be ignored.

MYTH 820. | *Antidepressant can cure depression.*

While antidepressants do help with treating depression, therapy is often necessary along with the medication to help a person overcome the disorder.

MYTH 821. | *You can snap out of a depression.*

People who suffer from depression can't simply snap out of it. Since it's a medical condition, people who suffer from the disorder must seek medical help.

MYTH 822. | *Depression happens after a sad situation.*

Depression isn't just an occasional bout of unhappiness due to death or a break up. Depression is diagnosed with unexplained periods of hopelessness, sadness and suicidal tendencies. These episodes come suddenly and inexplicably.

MYTH 823. | *Talking about depression will only make it worse.*

For a person who is suffering from depression, being left alone with their thoughts is much more harmful than talking to another individual about it. Having supportive, reliable and nonjudgmental listeners is crucial for the treatment of the disorder.

MYTH 824. | *Parrots naturally scream.* Parrots don't naturally scream, their owners teach them to scream because we react to them. Parrots quickly learn that when they scream, they get our attention, that's why they do it.

MYTH 825. | *Birth control pills make you gain weight.* In 2011, researchers at the Cochran Database System Review analyzed 49 studies that compared a variety of different birth control methods with placebos and found that birth control pills don't cause a woman to gain weight.

MYTH 826. | *You don't need to be on birth control if you're breastfeeding.* Breastfeeding can suppress the hormones from the pituitary gland that makes a woman ovulate, so while there's certainly a dip in a woman's fertility at that time, it's not as effective as the birth control pill.

MYTH 827. | *You have to take the birth control pill at the same time every day.* Despite the longstanding myth, the pill doesn't have to be taken at the same time every day. However, a lot of women use the same time every day technique so they can remember to take it.

MYTH 828. | *Taking the birth control pill for a long time will make it harder to get pregnant later on.* It's possible to get pregnant as soon as you stop taking the pill. While it can take 6 to 9 months for all of the hormones to leave your body, you can still get pregnant during this time.

MYTH 829. | *It's unhealthy to use birth control.* In order to be a good candidate for birth control, you have to be healthy in the first place. However, taking the pill won't affect your health in any way.

MYTH 830. | *Marijuana is physically addictive.* Less than 1% of people in the United States smoke marijuana more than once per day. An extremely low percentage of heavy users develop what appears to be a dependence but it's really a habit that they are having difficulty breaking as marijuana has no physical addiction.

MYTH 831. | *Penguins are not birds.* Penguins are actually a type of bird. To be more precise, penguins are a flightless bird of the Spheniscidae family.

MYTH 832. | *Penguins can breathe underwater.* Penguins are air breathers just like humans. However, they are extremely fast swimmers.

MYTH 833. | *Penguins don't have feathers.* Penguins, just like any other bird, have feathers. Also, they have an extremely efficient insulating layer right under a slick and water resistant layer of feathers.

MYTH 834. | *All penguins live in Antarctica.* More than 20 species of penguins live throughout the Southern Hemisphere, and there's even tropical species in the Galapagos.

MYTH 835. | *Nothing lives on glaciers.* Glaciers are a rich biological hotspot. Since they're very dusty places, the dust is bound together with rich and varied microbial life. such as cryoconite, which is a mixture of dust, bits of rock and microbes.

MYTH 836. | *Glaciers are white.* Glaciers come in many different colors such as, white, blue, grey, red, green and even black. Glacier ice is often blue but when snow falls, it forms a top layer, which is white.

MYTH 837. | *Cellphones are dangerous in hospitals.* A recent study done in 75 treatment rooms did 300 tests to see if there was interference between cellphones and hospital equipment, and found no evidence to support the claim.

MYTH 838. | *Eating disorders are a lifestyle choice.* Eating disorders are a serious and potentially life threatening mental illnesses. A person who has an eating disorder experiences severe disturbances in their behavior when it comes to eating and must seek medical attention.

MYTH 839. | *Dieting is a normal part of life.* While moderate and sustainable changes in diet and exercise are healthy, extreme dieting practices are not healthy nor are they a normal part of life.

MYTH 840. | *Water is blue because it reflects the sky.* Water looks blue because pure water is a blue chemical. The blue color is caused by the molecular structure as well as selective absorption and scattering of the light spectrum.

MYTH 841. | *The North Star is the brightest star.* Polaris, also known as the North Star, isn't the brightest star. The brightest star in the sky, apart from the Sun, is Sirius, located in the Canis Major constellation.

MYTH 842. | *Organic food production doesn't use pesticides.* Organic production can use "natural" pesticides, which include mineral salts and pesticides from planet based materials.

MYTH 843. | *In the United States, more than half of all farms are large corporate farms.* According to the Agriculture Council of America and the 2002 Agricultural Census, 94% of farms in the United States are operated by individuals or family corporations.

MYTH 844. | *Organic food production has less impact on the environment than traditional food production.* Many natural pesticides are still persistent in the environment and they have to be applied at higher rates than traditional pesticides in order to protect the crop.

MYTH 845. | *World hunger is caused by a worldwide shortage of food.* The world produces enough food to feed everyone but due to social, political and economic factors, food hunger is still a problem in our society.

MYTH 846. | *Dandruff is contagious.* Dandruff is not contagious, however, it could be hereditary.

MYTH 847. | *Dandruff can be cured.* Dandruff can't be cured but it can easily be controlled and prevented. Regular shampooing with dandruff shampoo and brushing can help with reducing the amount of dandruff you have.

MYTH 848. | *Dandruff isn't normal.* Dandruff affects over 50% of the world population.

MYTH 849. | *Washing your hair less will help with dandruff.* Actually, washing your hair regularly will help prevent and control dandruff. This doesn't mean that you should wash your hair every single day, but once every other day is a good idea.

MYTH 850. | *Dandruff can only happen on your scalp.* Dandruff can happen on any hair growing part of your body. However, it's most commonly occurring on the scalp.

MYTH 851. | *Ethanol pollutes the same as gasoline.* Ethanol actually has fewer greenhouse gas emissions than gasoline and is fully biodegradable.

MYTH 852. | *More energy goes into producing ethanol than it delivers as fuel.* Each gallon of ethanol produced from corn delivers one third or more energy than is used to produce it.

MYTH 853. | *Ethanol gasoline blends can lower fuel economy and can harm your engine.* Ethanol blends today have very little impact on fuel economy or vehicle performance.

MYTH 854. | *Setting realistic goals for weight loss is better than setting more ambitious goals.* Actually, recent studies suggest that people will generally lose more weight if they set more ambitious goals for themselves.

MYTH 855. | *Rapid weight loss is more likely to be regained.* Recent studies suggest that those who drop more weight quickly are more likely to weigh less years later.

MYTH 856. | *Physical education classes are important in the prevention and treatment of childhood obesity.* In their current form, physical education classes aren't long enough or intense enough to make a difference in the prevention and treatment of childhood obesity.

MYTH 857. | *Breastfeeding protects infants against obesity.* While breastfeeding does benefit the infant, there is no scientific data to suggest that it protects against obesity.

MYTH 858. | *Sex burns anywhere from 100 to 300 calories for each partner.* Intercourse lasts, on average, about six minutes and it burns just slightly more calories than sitting on the couch for six minutes.

MYTH 859. | *People who talk about suicide won't really go through with it.* The majority of people who commit or attempt suicide have given prior clue or warning.

MYTH 860. | *If a person is determined to kill himself or herself, nothing will stop them.* Actually, recent research into depressed and suicidal people has revealed that even the most severely depressed person has mixed feelings about death, often wavering until the very last moment between wanting to live and wanting to die.

MYTH 861. | *Talking about suicide will give the person the idea to do it.* If a person is already suicidal, you won't be giving them any more ideas than what they've already thought about. However, bringing up the topic and talking about it is one of the best things you can do for the person.

MYTH 862. | *All hamsters can share a cage.* While some hamsters can share a cage, others can't. The Syrian hamsters, for example, must never be caged together. They are extremely territorial and will fight to the death.

MYTH 863. | *Homemade juices contain all the fiber from the fruit.* Juice doesn't contain any fiber. The fiber component of most plants is what creates it's structure, when you juice the plant, you take away its structure and are left with its juice only.

MYTH 864. | *Homemade juice contains all the nutrients.* Whole fruit is loaded with dietary fiber to help digest the sugar and slow down the uptake of sugar into the bloodstream. In its whole form, we get the full array of its micronutrients and phytochemicals. When the fruit or plant is juiced, all of these things are stripped away from it.

MYTH 865. | *Certain diseases occur only in particular racial groups.* Actually, no disease is exclusive to one group even though certain diseases occur with increased frequency in particular racial groups.

MYTH 866. | *It's racist to base health care decisions on group identity.* Actually, since hypertension occurs more among black men, it would be appropriate to be more attentive to that possibility with a black male patient.

MYTH 867. | *There are no genetic differences between groups.* About 15% of human genetic variations differ between the various racial groups.

MYTH 868. | *A concussion only occurs as a result of a direct blow to the head.* A concussion may be caused by a direct blow to the head, face, neck or anywhere else on the body if the force of the impact is transmitted to the head.

MYTH 869. | *Only athletes in aggressive contact sports like football and hockey suffer concussions.* While football players have the highest number of concussions, concussions are also very common in hockey, lacrosse, wrestling, soccer, basketball and cheerleading.

MYTH 870. | *All concussions are the same.* The symptoms can vary a lot from person to person, depending on a variety of factors, including the degree of force and location of the impact, the degree of metabolic dysfunction, the tissue damage and recovery time, the number of previous concussions sustained by the athlete, and the time between injuries.

MYTH 871. | *A concussion occurs when a person experiences a loss of consciousness.* More than 95% of concussions do not result in a loss of consciousness.

MYTH 872. | *Carbohydrates make you fat.* Carbohydrates don't make you fat, excess calories make you fat. A person can cut all the carbohydrates they want, but if they're still eating excess calories, their body will store it as fat.

MYTH 873. | *St. Patrick brought Christianity to Ireland.* In 431, before St. Patrick began preaching in Ireland, Pope Celestine sent a bishop known as Palladius to convert the Irish into Christianity.

MYTH 874. | *St. Patrick banished snakes from the Emerald Isle.* Emerald Isle has been free of snakes throughout human history. Water that surrounded Ireland since the end of the last glacial period prevented snakes from slithering over and, before that, it was covered in ice and too cold for cold blooded creatures to live on.

MYTH 875. | *Green has historically been associated with St. Patrick's Day.* Knights in the Order of St. Patrick wore a color known as St. Patrick's Blue. The association to green dates back to the 18th century when supporters of Irish independence used the color to represent their cause.

MYTH 876. | *Muslims live in the Middle East.* The majority of Muslim people live in Asia, predominantly south and southeast Asia. More than 300 million Muslims live in Sub-Saharan Africa as well.

MYTH 877. | *All Muslims are Arabs.* An Arab is a person who speaks Arabic and only 20% of Muslims would fall into this category.

MYTH 878. | *Muslims don't believe in Jesus.* Muslims know and respect Jesus as a prophet of God. The Qur'an mentions Jesus 93 times, teaching that he performed miracles, was born of a virgin, and will return again as a Messiah.

MYTH 879. | *Islam oppresses women.* The often publicized oppression of women that happens in predominantly Islamic countries happens due to local customs and traditions not because of Islamic teachings and beliefs.

MYTH 880. | *Malaria exists everywhere in Southeast Asia.* Malaria in Southeast Asia exists primarily in the jungle and other forested areas. The urban centers are predominantly free of any malaria.

MYTH 881. | *Slavery is a direct product of capitalism.* Slavery goes as far back as the very first human records.

MYTH 882. | *Slavery is a product of Western civilization.* Actually, slavery is a universal institution that existed in almost every single large empire throughout our history.

MYTH 883. | *Slavery was always based on race.* Slavery hasn't been associated with people of African descent until the 15th century. Before then, all the races were used for slavery, whether they are poor and bought by noble people or if they were acquired through war.

MYTH 884. | *Europeans physically enslaved Africans or hired mercenaries to capture people for export.* Europeans didn't engage in slave raiding themselves. The majority of people who were transported to the Americas were enslaved and sold by Africans in Africa. In fact, many slave masters who sold black slaves to the Americas were black themselves.

MYTH 885. | *Kidnapping was the most common means of enslavement.* Actually, war was the most common source of enslavement.

MYTH 886. | *The majority of African slaves were imported into the United States.* Over 90% of slaves from Africa were imported into the Caribbean and South America.

MYTH 887. | *Europeans outnumbered Africans in the New World.* Before 1820, the number of Africans outnumbered European immigrants by 5 to 1.

MYTH 888. | *Slaves were only used for unskilled field labor.* Slave owners relied on slaves for skilled craftsmanship as the labor slaves performed required a very high skill level.

MYTH 889. | *Solar panels don't work on cloudy days.* On cloudy days the solar panels absorb less energy than they normally would but it doesn't mean that they wouldn't work at all.

MYTH 890. | *English Bulldogs can swim unassisted.* There is no way that an English Bulldog can hold itself above water with its short legs, large head and heavy body. However, they can swim if they have a life preserver on.

MYTH 891. | *Different countries see different phases of the Moon on the same day.* Everyone sees the same phases of the Moon. However, people that live south of the equator and face north to see the Moon, will see it upside down so that the reverse side of it is lit up.

MYTH 892. | *The Moon goes around the Earth in one day.* It takes about a month for the Moon to orbit the Earth.

MYTH 893. | *The Moon makes its own light like the Sun.* The Moon reflects the light of the Sun, just like other planets do.

MYTH 894. | *The Moon doesn't rotate.* The Moon spins on its axis, completing a rotation once every 27.3 days. The myth is due to the Moon taking the same period to orbit the Earth, keeping the same side facing us all the time.

MYTH 895. | *The Moon has no gravity.* The Moon does have gravity but due to its smaller size, it has only about one sixth of the Earth's gravity on its surface.

MYTH 896. | *The Moon is only visible at night.* We can also see the Moon during the day. However, when the moon is full, we wouldn't be able to see it during the day.

MYTH 897. | *Browser cookies track everything that you do online.* Almost all browser cookies are a session token that contain your login credentials to that particular website. All login credentials are encrypted and hashed by the website to make sure that they're protected.

MYTH 898. | *Browser cookies are viruses and spyware.* Cookies are just text files that aren't executed like viruses or spyware. While advertisers can use cookies to track which pop-up ads you've seen, the cookies have nothing to do with the advertisement in the first place.

MYTH 899. | *Che Guevara was celibate.* Che Guevara had six children with multiple women.

MYTH 900. | *Che Guevara was a poor Cuban man.* Che was born in Argentina and his parents were far from poor. His family was actually very wealthy and Che grew up with a very privileged upbringing.

MYTH 901. | *Che Guevara was a renegade.* Che was more of a geek than a renegade. He enjoyed playing chess, even entering a few local tournaments, enjoyed reading poetry, and excelled in math and engineering in school.

MYTH 902. | *Che Guevara wasn't book smart.* Che was highly book smart and even finished his medical degree. While in medical school, he concentrated on leprosy and how to help cure it.

MYTH 903. | *Che Guevara didn't travel much.* Actually, he travelled extensively and even lived in many foreign countries. In 1964, he even spoke at the United Nations.

MYTH 904. | *Weightlifting is bad for your joints.* A study that was published in the Journal of Rheumatology found that people who suffered from knee joint pain and who performed weight bearing exercises, experienced a 43% reduction in pain after four months. Strength training can help keep the structures around your joints strong, which better supports them.

MYTH 905. | *Weightlifting causes high blood pressure.* Weightlifting can lower both systolic and diastolic blood pressure by 2-4%. According to the American Heart Association, you would be able to see benefits with just 2-3 sessions a week.

MYTH 906. | *Weightlifting decreases flexibility.* A study in the Journal of Strength & Conditioning Research found that resistance training improves flexibility as well as static stretching.

MYTH 907. | *Homosexual people are promiscuous.* Homosexual people are just as likely to be promiscuous as heterosexual people. Promiscuity has nothing to do with sexual orientation, it's purely based on each individual person.

MYTH 908. | *Marijuana prohibition protects kids.* In 2011, 1 in every 15 high school students in the United States reported that they smoke almost every single day. This is the first time that the United States had more teenagers smoking marijuana than cigarettes.

MYTH 909. | *Holland and Portugal have legalized marijuana use.* Holland never legalized marijuana but, they do have a policy in place since 1976 which doesn't enforce existing laws against possession for about 700 small coffee shops which sell very small amounts. However, growing and distributing marijuana is still illegal in Holland. Portugal has decriminalized all drugs, but the acquisition, possession and use of marijuana can still be punished with fines and community service.

MYTH 910. | *Prisons are full of people who were charged with marijuana possession.* Actually, 99% of prisoners in the United States who were sent to prison with marijuana related charges were sent in because of distribution and not possession. Only 1% of people were sent in for possession.

MYTH 911. | *Smoking marijuana is completely harmless.* Heavy marijuana use can be harmful. Marijuana smoke, chemically, is very similar to tobacco smoke and heavy smokers are still at risk for the same type of negative health effects as cigarette smokers.

MYTH 912. | *Marijuana is dangerous.* Actually, quite a few studies have found that marijuana is much less harmful than alcohol and tobacco.

MYTH 913. | *William Shakespeare was well educated.* Shakespeare only went to school as a child and didn't go to university like other upper class children. It was during his time in school as a child that he learned how to read and write.

MYTH 914. | *William Shakespeare was a full time writer.* Actually, Shakespeare was a full time actor and he performed in many theatre groups, such as the Lord Chamberlain's Men.

MYTH 915. | *William Shakespeare was alive during the Elizabethan period.* Most of Shakespeare's work was performed during the Jacobean era and then changed as the times changed to other more dramatic satire.

MYTH 916. | *William Shakespeare wrote all of his plays by himself.* Shakespeare often collaborated with other writers for his plays. A man by the name of George Wilkins worked on many plays with Shakespeare and is believed to have wrote the first half of Pericles.

MYTH 917. | *Heroin is less dangerous when smoked or snorted.* Heroin is deadly no matter what way you ingest it into your body.

MYTH 918. | *Heroin users become addicted instantly after using the drug.* Heroin takes months or even longer of continual use to get addicted to the drug.

MYTH 919. | *Beer and wine don't get you as drunk as mixed drinks.* A glass of wine, a bottle of beer and a shot of vodka or any other distilled spirit contain the same amount of alcohol.

MYTH 920. | *Drinking alcohol makes you fat.* While alcohol does have calories, studies done on their effects show that there isn't any significant weight gain attributed to it. The main causes of weight gain happen to fall on the lifestyle and genetics of the person.

MYTH 921. | *The United States has the heaviest drinkers in the world.* In 2011, the World Health Organization reported the top 10 alcohol consuming countries in the world and all of them were in Europe, with the top 9 being located in Eastern Europe.

MYTH 922. | *A large meal before drinking helps you stay sober.* A full stomach doesn't prevent the absorption of alcohol into your bloodstream, it just slows the entire process down.

MYTH 923. | *Alcohol kills brain cells.* Alcohol has no effect on your brain cells and, recently, researchers have found that red wine helps the brain and can prevent dementia in old age.

MYTH 924. | *Dark beer has higher alcohol content than light beer.* The color of the beer doesn't indicate the amount of alcohol in the beer.

MYTH 925. | *Deleting files off your computer means that they are gone forever.* The majority of files that you have deleted off your computer can be recovered if you begin the recovery process early enough.

MYTH 926. | *All magnets can destroy your hard drive.* An extremely powerful magnet can erase a hard drive, but it won't destroy it.

MYTH 927. | *Restarting computer will be bad for your computer in the long run.* Restarting your computer won't damage it at all and is actually beneficial to keep it running smoothly.

MYTH 928. | *In space, you can hear sounds.* In space, there is no atmosphere through which vibrations could pass, therefore, no sound would be heard.

MYTH 929. | *The Battle of Bunker Hill in the United States was fought on Bunker Hill.* Actually, the Battle of Bunker Hill was fought on Breed's Hill, which is nearby.

MYTH 930. | *All cowboys where white in the Old West.* There was plenty of black cowboys in the Old West. Some researchers suggest that it was as common as 1 in every 3 cowboys.

MYTH 931. | *General Custer died at the battle of Little Bighorn.* Custer had been demoted to Lieutenant Colonel approximately 10 years before the battle, therefore, he died as Lieutenant Colonel Custer and not General Custer.

MYTH 932. | *President William Henry Harrison died because he didn't wear a coat while giving a long inauguration speech in the cold.* President William Henry Harrison got sick three weeks after his inauguration and it wasn't due to the cold.

MYTH 933. | *Everyone died in the Hindenburg disaster.* Actually, 62 out of the 97 passengers survived the explosion and crash.

MYTH 934. | *The Liberty Bell was a cherished piece in the early years of the United States.* The Liberty Bell was sold as scrap metal in 1828 at a discounted rate but the deal fell through when the person who bought the bell decided that it wasn't worth the effort.

MYTH 935. | *The sinking of the Lusitania in 1914 directly lead to the United States getting involved in World War I.* The sinking of the Lusitania didn't lead the United States to get involved in World War I because they didn't enter the war until 1917, 3 years after the incident.

MYTH 936. | *Peter Minuit bought Manhattan from the Canarsee Indians for $24.* There wasn't any money exchanged between Minuit and the Canarsee Indians. Some trinkets might have been exchanged between the two groups but no record exists of any transaction taking place.

MYTH 937. | *The New York City blackout in 1965 led to an increase in birthrate nine months later.* The blackout in 1965 didn't lead to an increase in the birthrate nine months later because the birth rate was very similar to the previous rates at that time of the year.

MYTH 938. | *The Pilgrims who landed on the Mayflower in 1620 were the first English settlers in the United States.* The Pilgrims weren't the first English settlers as Jamestown in Virginia, and other surrounding settlements, were established as early as 1607.

MYTH 939. | *The United States was the first country to allow women to vote.* While the United States ratified the 19th Amendment in 1920, it wasn't the first country to allow women to vote. The first country to allow women to vote was New Zealand, which did it in 1893.

MYTH 940. | *Scalping originated with American Indians.* Scalping originated in Europe and was introduced to the Indians when the white colonists offered rewards for the scalp of other Indians.

MYTH 941. | *Americans fought under the Stars and Stripes flag during the Revolutionary War.* Though the myth is found on many famous paintings, the first time American soldiers fought under the Star and Stripes flag was the Mexican-American War in 1846, well after the Revolutionary War.

MYTH 942. | *Tomahawks were thrown by Native Americans in battle.* Tomahawks were very valuable to Naive Americans and weren't thrown, they were only used as a club.

MYTH 943. | *Ants are working all the time.* Ants only work about one fifth of their life. They only seem busy because the ant colony stays busy throughout the day.

MYTH 944. | *All armadillos roll into a ball when attacked.* Only a South American species of armadillo rolls into a ball when its attacked. North American armadillos run away or dig themselves into the ground when attacked or when they feel threatened.

MYTH 945. | *The Australian Shepherd dog originated in Australia.* The Australian Shepherd dog actually originated in California, United States.

MYTH 946. | *Bears hibernate.* Bears don't hibernate, they become dormant, which is very similar to sleeping. Their temperature, heart rate, and breathing don't slow down like an animal's who is hibernating would.

MYTH 947. | *Beavers use their tails to compress mud while building dams.* Beavers don't use their tails to compress mud while building dams, they use it to slap the water's surface in order to warn other beavers of incoming danger.

MYTH 948. | *Bloodhounds get their name because they use blood to track humans.* Bloodhounds got their name from the tradition of keeping breeding records, which document their bloodlines.

MYTH 949. | *Boa constrictors crush their victims to death.* Boa constrictors actually constrict the breathing of their victims, which causes them to suffocate.

MYTH 950. | *Buffalo roamed the prairies of North America.* Buffalo never roamed the prairies of North America, those were bison. They were called buffalo because they reminded the European immigrants of water buffalo from Asia and Africa.

MYTH 951. | *Catgut comes from cats.* Catgut, which is used for making stringed instruments, doesn't come from cats, but from sheep and horses.

MYTH 952. | *A chicken is considered a flightless bird.* Chickens can actually fly for a short period of time. The longest recorded flight was for 13 seconds.

MYTH 953. | *Cows can't walk down stairs.* Cows can be led up or down stairs.

MYTH 954. | *All crows are black.* Actually, Brazil's crimson fruit crow is a bright shade of red.

MYTH 955. | *You can tell the age of a male deer by the number of points on its antler.* The antlers on a male deer grow each year and the number of points is dependent on its genetic makeup and overall health, and it has nothing to do with the deer's age.

MYTH 956. | *Earwigs crawl into ears.* Actually, they're called earwigs because their hind legs look like an ear, and they don't crawl into ears.

MYTH 957. | *Flying fish can fly.* Flying fish don't actually fly, they just propel themselves out of the water and glide.

MYTH 958. | *French Poodles originated in France.* Actually, French Poodles originated in Germany.

MYTH 959. | *Goats eat tin cans.* Goats don't eat tin cans, they may nibble on them if it's in their way but they won't actually swallow one.

MYTH 960. | *The most common use for a guinea pig is as a pet or as a test subject.* Actually, the most common use for them is to be eaten in South American countries, where they originated from.

MYTH 961. | *Hens sit on their eggs.* Hens don't sit on their eggs, they squat with most of their weight on their legs, otherwise they would crush the egg.

MYTH 962. | *Horned toads are toads.* Horned toads are actually lizards and not toads.

MYTH 963. | *Hornets are more dangerous than bees and wasps.* Actually, hornets aren't that aggressive and they will rarely sting. Even if they do sting you, their sting is only life threatening if the person is allergic to the hornet's poison.

MYTH 964. | *All mammals are monogamous.* Only about 3% of mammals are monogamous.

MYTH 965. | *Monkeys are looking for insects when they pick at the skin of other monkeys.* Actually, they're looking for salty bits of loose skin and not insects.

MYTH 966. | *Mules are the same as donkeys.* Mules aren't the same as donkeys as they're the offspring of a male donkey and a female horse.

MYTH 967. | *The painting of the Mona Lisa is called the "Mona Lisa".* Leonardo da Vinci's famous paintings is actually called "La Gioconda."

MYTH 968. | *All great painters became famous after their death.* The majority of master painters, such as Michelangelo and Leonardo da Vinci, were very well known while they were alive and were also in high demand.

MYTH 969. | *El Greco, the famous painter, was Spanish.* El Greco wasn't Spanish, he was Greek, and his name was just a nickname describing his nationality. His real name was Domenikos Theotokopoulous.

MYTH 970. | *Pablo Picasso always painted abstract art.* Picasso painted professionally for 10 years before he became interested in cubism and began painting abstract art.

MYTH 971. | *All Greek sculptures were white.* The majority of Greek sculptures were originally painted with different colors but, over time, the colors peeled off and only left the white base underneath.

MYTH 972. | *Being in the tail sections of the airplane is the most dangerous place to be during a plane crash.* Actually, the people in the tail section have a 40% greater chance of surviving than other passengers.

MYTH 973. | *The Wright Brothers' plane was called the "Kitty Hawk".* Kitty Hawk was the name of the town where the 1903 flight was held. The actual plane was called the "Wright Flyer."

MYTH 974. | *The Heinz Company had exactly 57 verities.* Actually, the Heinz Company never had 57 verities, the number was completely made up.

MYTH 975. | *Walt Disney's signature is used as the company logo.* The famous signature was made by a company artist and didn't resemble Walt Disney's signature at all.

MYTH 976. | *Bottles of aspirin have cotton in them to ensure freshness.* The wads of cotton that you find in aspirin bottles are there to prevent the tablets from breaking if the bottle is dropped.

MYTH 977. | *Banana oil comes from bananas.* Banana oil is petroleum oil that just has a scent that's similar to a banana.

MYTH 978. | *The Barbie doll originated in the United States.* The Barbie doll originated in Germany and was created by the Mattel Company as a gag for stag parties.

MYTH 979. | *Boomerangs were originally made to be returned to the thrower.* The original boomerangs were used in war and hunting to kill a target from a distance and wasn't meant to return back to the thrower.

MYTH 980. | *Diamonds are the most valuable gem.* Actually, rubies sell for about 4 to 5 times the cost of diamonds.

MYTH 981. | *Diamonds rings were always given as engagement rings.* Diamond rings began being custom for engagement rings after the 1930s, when a diamond company worked with Hollywood to glamorize the idea.

MYTH 982. | *Electric fans cool the room.* Electric fans actually don't cool the room, the room just feels cooler because the fan blows the warm air radiated by your body away from your skin. Leaving an electric fan in an empty room, therefore, is a waste of energy.

MYTH 983. | *Clouds don't have any weight.* Actually, researchers argue that clouds weigh, on average, 500 tons.

MYTH 984. | *The Sun is constantly on fire.* The Sun is actually fusing hydrogen atoms into helium, which gives off energy that will last for another 4 billion years.

MYTH 985. | *Going from one star system to another only takes a few days.* It would take tens of thousands of years for our fastest space probe to reach the next nearest star.

MYTH 986. | *The tails of comets always flow behind them.* Actually, bright comets have two tails, one of dust peeling off the melting snow and dirt that's in the heart of the comment, and the second one of plasma being vented by the comet's heart.

MYTH 987. | *Galaxies are too far away to be seen.* While galaxies are very far away, even a small telescope can reveal basic structure in galaxies like the Whirlpool Galaxy. The problem with seeing far away galaxies isn't their distance, it's the fact that in today's world, it's very difficult to find a sky that is dark enough.

MYTH 988. | *Satellites aren't affected by Earth's gravity.* Gravity is what makes the satellites orbit. If the gravity didn't affect satellites, once a probe was launched into space, it would simply move away from the planet at a constant speed in a straight line.

MYTH 989. | *Visible light is the only light that exists.* Actually, there are other forms of light which you can't see. For example, heat is a form of infrared light that you can feel and ultraviolet light can else be felt as heat hitting your skin when you're outside in the Sun.

MYTH 990. | *There is only one type of amnesia.* There is a second form of amnesia called anterograde amnesia in which you can remember everything that happened in your past but you can't form any new long-term memories.

MYTH 991. | *You should never comfort a crying baby.* Recent studies suggest that, for the first few months of a baby's life, you should always console it. After, it won't do any harm to comfort a crying baby.

MYTH 992. | *It's possible to multi-task.* Your brain can only engage in one cognitive task at a time. That means that for every extra thing that you try to add simply makes it harder for your brain to work efficiently and effectively.

MYTH 993. | *Psychologists can read minds.* Though psychologists are very skilled at understanding human behavior, it doesn't mean that they're capable of reading anyone's mind. In fact, psychologists often say that the human mind is so complex that they often have trouble reading their own mind.

MYTH 994. | *Boys and girls don't have unique gender characteristics at birth.* Boys and girls do have unique gender characteristics at birth that are different in both physical and hormonal respects. The difference in physical and hormonal characteristics is what affects their inclinations and behavior.

MYTH 995. | *Over stimulating a baby will make it more intelligent.* After numerous tests, researchers have found that the vocabulary development of children who had not watched Little Einstein videos was in fact slightly better than the children who did. In fact, child psychologists insist that the best way to help a baby develop an intelligent mind is with one on one contact with parents.

MYTH 996. | *Many people experience a midlife crisis in their 40s or 50s.* Studies done in various cultures have come to the conclusion that middle age isn't a particularly stressful or difficult period in a person's life. On the contrary, people aged 40 to 60 are found to be more in control of their lives and emotions than younger people.

MYTH 997. | *When a person is dying, they pass through universal series of psychological stages.* Dying is different for every single person. There is no one universal way that a person dies.

MYTH 998. | *It's common for people to repress the memories of traumatic experiences.* Research shows that people remember traumatic events, such as natural disasters or instances of rape, very well. They will remember disturbing flashbacks with almost crystal clear quality.

MYTH 999. | *When taking a test, if you're unsure of your answer, it's best to stick with your initial gut feeling.* Actually it's best not to trust our instincts when taking a test. If you have a good reason to believe that you're wrong, you should use your head and not your gut feeling.

MYTH 1000. | *People can learn information while asleep.* People can't learn information while asleep because the brain uses that opportunity to organize the information that you have acquired throughout the day. For people who listen to a person narrating important information to them while they sleep, it would be much more effective to do it while you're fully awake.

Made in the USA
Columbia, SC
13 December 2019

84832719R00117